# The New World Order and the Eugenics Wars: a Christian Perspective

Thanks Kellie!

# The New World Order and the Eugenics Wars: a Christian Perspective

Andrew John Hoffman

First Edition

The New World Order and the Eugenics Wars: a Christian Perspective



www.eugenicswars.com ; andrew@eugenicswars.com



Cover art and design by David Dees

Printed by Believers Press

ISBN: 978-0-578-04162-9

Scripture taken from the New King James Version.

# Table of Contents

This book would not have been written if it were not for the inspiration and encouragement of Chris White. Chris, your work helped me see clearly when I was confused and struggling with these subjects for the first time. Thank you, brother.

# Introduction

God exists. Satan exists. The Bible is the inspired Word of God. Jesus Christ left his place in heaven at the right hand of God to come to earth. He then lived, taught, suffered, died, and bore the full brunt of the wrath of God for my sake and for yours. Our only reason for hope is that Jesus Christ not only conquered death but that through him alone we are offered reconciliation with God. If your faith is placed somewhere else other than in the Lord Jesus Christ, then I cannot recommend that you read this book. The information that I have discovered and that I will share in this book will shake your sense of reality and can lead some very dangerous places if you are not grounded in faith and trust in Christ Jesus our Lord.

This book is an account of my own awakening. It is my prayer that God will use this book to wake up my brothers and sisters in Christ. This book is a call to wake up from our media-induced fake reality. This book is a call to action. It is a call to truly believe what we claim to believe and to act on those beliefs. We claim to believe in a God who is good and Satan who is evil, yet we too often accept relativistic arguments denying even the existence of good and evil. Or, perhaps even more damagingly, we deny the role of any actors in the universe other than God. We have been convinced, perhaps by media caricatures of a tailed red man with a pitchfork, that although Satan may be real, he is powerless to affect anything. The logical consequence of this belief, whether explicitly or implicitly held, is to fail to resist evil. The further consequence is to live lives of narcissistic legalism in which our obsession with our own problems, circumstances, and sin keeps us from what Jesus has called us to do. Jesus Christ has called us to lives of servant love and warrior prayer to bring the Kingdom of God to people who are currently enmeshed, entangled, and bound in the kingdoms of Satan.

We live in enemy territory. Satan is called the "ruler of this world" by Jesus[1] and is seen actively striving against Jesus both directly[2] in the wilderness and indirectly through Peter.[3] It is important to realize that Satan did not tempt Jesus to do things we typically associate with sin; Satan tried to get Jesus to seize power through political means and to take a shortcut past the cross. Of course, while this would have resulted in much better living conditions here on earth (a just society, etc.), our sins would still have no payment. We would have to pay the consequences of sin—eternal damnation and separation from God, ourselves. By taking the wrath of God for every single sin on himself[4] and then being resurrected, Jesus has conquered the power of both sin and death.

Through his death and resurrection, Jesus conquered death and showed that he is the rightful ruler of humanity. But, Christ does not yet rule the world. Satan still controls the political kingdoms and systems of this world. This will continue until Christ returns and claims his rightful authority over mankind. Until then, however, we truly do live in enemy territory. A cursory glance at world events both current and historic shows that the power systems of this world are the opposite of Christ-like. In fact, they are satanic to their core. This book is about those systems of power and how Satan manipulates the minds of mankind in order to control us. More importantly, this book is a call to resist the satanic order that Satan's minions call the New World Order. Of course, as with all things coming from the Great Deceiver, it is not a "new" order, but an ancient system of bloodthirsty oppression.

This is also a book about my own awakening to a way of looking at the world that was unknown to me just a few years ago. For me, it was a sudden and shocking experience to realize

---

1 John 12:31, John 14:30, and John 16:11

2 Luke 4:1-13

3 Matthew 16:23

4 Chuck Missler asserts that in some real way, Jesus has to suffer for eternity outside of this time domain to pay the full penalty of our sins. 66/40 Radio Broadcast from Koinonia House www.khouse.org

that I had been viewing the world from a fraudulent point of view and that my beliefs were based on false assumptions. As I have been researching these topics over the past couple of years, I have been amazed at the lies I have believed for much of my life. I have seen clearly how believing the lies that I have believed have led me to sin and to doubt God.

For many of you, the information in this book will make you angry. It will activate cognitive dissonance that will cause you to want to deny that these things are real and that the beliefs you have held are in many cases false. It is my prayer, however, that you will find that the genuine pursuit of truth always leads back to God and his Word. My faith has been strengthened immensely by the realization that the same deep analysis that reveals the lies that create the mainstream reality also reveals that the Bible can be trusted completely. The governments and systems of men in this world may rightly fear questioning truth-seekers, but God welcomes them.

In each chapter and topic in this book, it is my goal to give basic information that is well-supported by sound evidence. I will also try to point the reader in the direction of sources of information that contain deeper and more comprehensive research and evidence. There are people far more qualified than I am to explicate any one of the individual topics. What I attempt to provide, however, is a general and cohesive picture of the world we live in and the factors at work within it. In my own life I have often felt a deep disconnect between the lens through which I viewed the world and the world as it is presented in the Bible. It is my belief that we live in the midst of a spiritual battle between God and Satan. Each of us has contributions that Jesus has called us to make to the bringing of the Kingdom of God to our world. Satan, being unable to take away our salvation, focuses instead on keeping us neutralized and inactive. It is my prayer that the information presented in this book will allow you to see the world as it is more clearly and to see clearly the role that God calls us to play in his ultimate victory over sin, death, and Satan himself.

# Chapter 1
## Reality?

We live in a world of mass-media sound bites and slogans. We would like to believe our media intake has little or no impact on our lives or on our view of reality. Studies have shown that most people believe advertising works on other people but not on them.[1] I want to make the argument that we *are* in fact impacted by what we see, hear, read, and otherwise consume in this age of information. I also want to make the argument that all media, not just advertising, is intentional.

Our view of reality has been shaped, molded, and warped by those who manipulate what our minds are exposed to on a daily basis.[2] Much of what we believe about the world is communicated to us through intermediate means rather than direct experience. Those of us who claim to be Christians would like to say that our media intake has less of an effect on our belief systems than the Bible, but is that really the case? I would argue that our "Christian" beliefs have been compartmentalized and are in many cases only a small factor in how we see the world as a whole. Do we look for spiritual causes for events or have we bought into the materialistic mindset—almost completely unique to the post-enlightenment western world— that claims all things can be explained "scientifically?"

1 O'Sullivan, Jeremiah R. "The Social and Cultural Effects of Advertising." http://www.crvp.org/book/Series05/V-4/chapter_vi.htm

2 In theory, of course, we can choose to avoid mass media. However, unless you're living in a cabin in the woods somewhere far from civilization with no television, radio, or internet then mass media has a real effect on your mind.

Do we view the world the way Jesus did? Do we view the world the way it truly is? Despite our claims of being well-informed, we really have no clue about what is going on in this world if we allow the world to shape our view of it.

Jesus focused his ministry on bringing the Kingdom of God to our world.[3] Although Jesus came to bring the Kingdom of God to the world, he makes it clear that his kingdom is not *of* this world: "*Jesus answered, 'My kingdom is not of this world. If My kingdom were of this world, My servants would fight, so that I should not be delivered to the Jews; but now My kingdom is not from here.*'"[4] Jesus made it clear that the Kingdom of God is much different than the kingdoms of this world when he said in the Beatitudes, "*Blessed are you poor, for yours is the Kingdom of God.*"[5] The kingdoms of this world belong to the wealthy, not the poor. If we want to experience the Kingdom of God and bring it to the people around us, we must first realize that it is not a political kingdom of the world and cannot be achieved through worldly kingdom tactics.

Jesus viewed disease, ignorance, pride, and even stormy weather as being demonically influenced.[6] The ministry of Jesus targeted both the physical and spiritual needs that the people around him had. Oftentimes, Jesus' first response when someone was brought to him for healing from physical ailments was to forgive their sins.[7] This shows that Jesus placed a higher priority on the condition of our souls than our bodies. Satan and his minions often use illness or any number of other negative circumstances to distract us from issues of greater significance in the spiritual realm. God, however, is constantly working through even the worst of our circumstances to show us our need for Him and to draw us closer to Him through meeting our needs.

In order to be effective messengers of the Kingdom of God, it is important for us to view the world accurately. We must seek to see God, ourselves and others, Satan, sin, creation, etc, through the perspective of Jesus Christ, and not through the deceptive lens of our own selfish worldview which is easily manipulated by

3 "Kingdom of God" is found 32 times in the gospels alone.

4 John 18:36

5 Luke 6:20

6 Mark 3:9-15, Matthew 8:26-34, Matthew 23, etc.

7 Mark 2:5-12

Satan. Jesus viewed Satan as a personal entity and adversary capable of influencing even his closest friends.[8] In modern, Western Christianity, we tend to view Satan as cartoonishly irrelevant—if we consider him at all. As Charles Baudelaire wrote, "the greatest trick the devil ever pulled was convincing the world he does not exist." Christians of a deterministic persuasion view all events as being orchestrated straight from the hand of God, no matter how heinous and evil they may be. I would argue that, as C.S. Lewis says, "Real Christianity goes much nearer to Dualism than people think."[9] Satan, of course, is infinitely lesser than Jesus Christ. In fact, it seems Biblically accurate to identify his strength as more nearly the same as Michael or Gabriel. However, for a finite amount of time in this finite place, Satan has been granted a great deal of authority and has chosen to use that authority to seek worship and glory for himself instead of serving God.[10]

Satan desires worship from men and power over them. He is not omnipresent or omnipotent and must use deception, technology, and the manipulation of hierarchical systems of political control in order to wield power over humanity. Satan is a master of human psychology, of appealing to our pride, and of appealing to our sin nature. His oldest lie is that we can become gods ourselves. If, that is, we will only stop obeying God and start relying on our own wisdom and ability to discern good from evil to shape the world.[11] From the Garden of Eden to the current New Age movement, the lie has remained the same.

Jesus knew that Satan could only offer lies and counterfeits of the true authority that God had given Him. When Satan offered Jesus the kingdoms of this world in exchange for His worship, Jesus refused.

> Then the devil, taking Him up on a high mountain, showed Him all the kingdoms of the world in a moment of time. And the devil said to Him, "All this authority I will give You, and their glory; for this has been delivered to me, and I give it to whomever I wish.

8 Matthew 16:23

9 C.S. Lewis in *Mere Christianity*.

10 Greg Boyd's book *Satan and the Problem of Evil* covers this issue in much greater depth.

11 Genesis 3:4-5

> Therefore, if You will worship before me, all will be Yours." And Jesus answered and said to him, "Get behind Me, Satan! For it is written, 'You shall worship the Lord your God, and Him only you shall serve.'[12]

Jesus refused to take a false shortcut around the cross. This passage does make you wonder, however, if Satan has made similar offers to world leaders throughout history.

Jesus claimed the right to rule through His death and resurrection. He has not yet begun to overtly reign, however, choosing instead to plant the "mustard seed" of the Kingdom of God. Even though Jesus Christ is not yet on the political thrones of this world, He has made it possible for His followers to experience the Kingdom of God here and now. We are to be in the world, but not of the world.[13] We are not to "buy in" to the systems of this world, because from a Biblical perspective, Satan is in charge of them.

Should we trust what the media tells us? Does modern man's view of reality match up with the Biblical portray of reality, with the reality that Jesus lived in and of which He was constantly aware? The world around us, as it is presented to us in the media, is not the whole of reality. In fact, it is meant to distract and keep us from reality. Once we realize this, we can begin to analyze the messages that bombard us on a daily basis for what they are, satanic propaganda. Virtually any time we turn on the TV, look at a billboard, open a newspaper, or surf the Internet, we are being lied to. If we agree that Satan is both the father of lies and the prince of this world,[14] we should not be surprised that in spite of our best intentions, we believe a lot of things that are simply untrue. It is crucial for us to be humble enough to admit when we have been deceived. So, that we can see through Satan's deception, and work to thwart his agenda while we work to further the Kingdom of God, in anticipation of the return of our Lord and Savior Jesus Christ.

Satan's agenda is to build a world government structure that is capable of being ruled by very few people that can control the

12 Luke 4:5-9

13 John 17:14-16

14 John 8:44

life of each individual on the planet.[15] Satan uses many tricks to get people to carry out his agenda, but the main levers he uses are the promises of money and power. Satan's minions include bankers, bureaucrats, generals, and politicians. Virtually all of those at the top levels (humanly speaking), are also Luciferians and occultists. All of us who willingly participate in systems of hierarchical and compartmentalized control serve Satan's agenda. Political power is the power to rule over another person against their will.[16] This is the power that Satan craves, and this is the power that Satan's minions are collecting and exercising in doing the bidding of their mammon master.

Despite Satan's best efforts, however, he will ultimately be utterly defeated. Until that time, the battle between the servants of the one true God and the servants of Satan will continue.

15 While the claim that this is Satan's agenda is unique to a Christian perspective, the fact that there is a drive for the creation of world government can be verified from hundreds of secular sources. One must-see interview is the late Aaron Russo discussing what Nick Rockefeller told him about the agenda of the elite. *Reflections and Warnings, an interview with Aaron Russo* is a documentary film that contains the entire interview. Most of the interview (conducted by Alex Jones) included in this film is available for free on the Internet.
16 Please read Ron Paul's excellent article on this subject, titled "Political Power and the Rule of Law." http://www.lewrockwell.com/paul/paul366.html

# Chapter 2

# Good and Evil: The Battle until the Time of Christ Incarnate

In Genesis, we read that God created the entire universe in six days, and on the seventh day, God rested.[1] Modern physics declares the age of the universe to be approximately 15 billion years. My working thesis is that good science and a straightforward reading of the Bible will not contradict each other, so how can this be? We seemingly must reject either the science or the Bible or try to manipulate one to fit the other. Gerald Schroeder, an MIT trained physicist and scholar of the Torah, argues that there is another option. Schroeder first asserts that the Genesis account looks from the perspective of the beginning of the universe—until man, the climax and pinnacle of creation, is created and the perspective shifts to that of a conscious and aware humanity. Here is part of his argument:

> Each day of creation is numbered. Yet there is discontinuity in the way the days are numbered. The verse says: "There is evening and morning, Day One." But the second day does not say "evening and morning, Day Two." Rather, it says "evening and morning, a second day." And the Torah continues with this pattern: "Evening and morning, a third day... a fourth day... a fifth day... the sixth day." Only on the first day does the text use a different form: not "first day," but "Day One" ("Yom Echad"). Many English translations make the mistake of writing "a first day." That is because editors want things to be nice and consistent. But they throw out the cosmic message in the text! There is a qualitative difference, as Nahmanides says, between "one" and "first." One is absolute; first is comparative. The Torah could not write "a first day" on the first day because there had not yet been a second

1 Genesis 1:1-2:2

> day relative to it. Had the perspective of the Bible for the first six days been from Sinai looking back, the Torah would have written a first day. The perspective of the Bible for the six days of Genesis is from the beginning looking forward. At the creation of Adam and Eve, the soul of humanity, the Bible perspective switches to Earth based time.[2]

This shift in perspective may seem insignificant until we consider what Einstein taught us, that time is relative. When physicists declare the age of the universe is 15 billion years, what they are really saying is that the age of the universe is 15 billion years as measured from Earth when we look back to the creation of matter and time, the "Big Bang." Schroeder then uses the analogy of sending out a laser beam in one second bursts simultaneously with the creation of matter and time. Because the universe is expanding, the bursts of light would not be one second apart when we see them here on Earth. In fact, they may be billions of years apart.

Thanks to modern physics, the rate of expansion of the universe and the corresponding effect on time is now calculable. Schroeder explains this calculation and its implications as follows:

> The general relationship between time near the beginning and time today is a million million. That is a 1 with 12 zeros after it. So when a view from the beginning looking forward says "I'm sending you a pulse every second," would we see it every second? No. We would see it every million million seconds. That is the stretching effect of the expansion of the universe.
>
> The Talmud tells us that the soul of Adam was created at five and a half days after the beginning of the calendar. That is a half day before the termination of the sixth day. At that moment the cosmic calendar ceases and an Earth based calendar starts. . How would we see those days stretched by a million million? The million million expansion of five and a half days gives an age of the universe as 15 billion years. NASA gives a value of about 14 billion years. Considering the many approximations, and that the Bible works with only six periods of time, the agreement to within a few percent is in my opinion extraordinary.
>
> The five and a half days of Genesis are not of equal duration. Each time the universe doubles in size, the perception of time halves as we project that time back toward the beginning of the universe.

2 Gerald Schroeder, "The Age of the Universe" http://www.geraldschroeder.com/AgeUniverse.aspx

> The rate of doubling, that is the fractional rate of change, is very rapid at the beginning and decreases with time simply because as the universe gets larger and larger, even though the actual expansion rate is approximately constant, it takes longer and longer for the overall size to double. Because of this, the earliest of the six days have most of the 15 billion years sequestered with them.[3]

In other words, the Bible is validated, not refuted, by modern science. This issue is important because in this book I seek to take the Bible seriously. That does not mean always literally, but it does mean not trying to explain away what the Bible clearly says because it appears to contradict our modern materialistic perspective. The brief history that I outline in this chapter and the next is an attempt at a Biblically-sound intentional view of history with a focus on areas of history and scripture not often discussed in mainline churches.

Lucifer, one of the most powerful and beautiful of God's created angels, decides that he is worthy of worship and rebels against God. God, who has previously granted Lucifer limited dominion over the Earth for a limited time, does not rescind Lucifer's power even though Lucifer has rebelled against him. Although God does not rescind Lucifer's power, it is Adam to whom God entrusts dominion over creation.[4]

Satan tempts Eve to eat of the fruit of the tree of the knowledge of good and evil.[5] As Greg Boyd points out in his book *Repenting of Religion*, humanity fell when we chose through eating of this fruit to become judges of good and evil rather than living in innocence and obedience to God. Only God can be lover and judge. Fallen humanity is confined to loving to the extent that we do not judge, and judging to the extent that we do not love.[6]

---

3 Gerald Schroeder, "The Age of the Universe" http://www.geraldschroeder.com/AgeUniverse.aspx [Incidentally, it is not my intention to argue for or against the validity of the Talmud. The fact that modern physics places the age of the universe within the range of the value of the sixth day is quite significant.]

4 Genesis 1:15-20

5 Genesis 3

6 Greg Boyd, *Repenting of Religion*. The prohibition on judging means that we do not get to decide for ourselves what is right and wrong. Our discernment must always be based on God's Word and guided by the Holy Spirit.

Satan's promise was a truth covered lie. Adam and Eve were now capable of knowing good and evil and judging themselves, but with this knowledge came sin's ever present companion, hiddenness and shame.[7] God's curse to the satanic serpent includes the following, "I will put enmity between you and the woman, and between your seed and her Seed; He shall bruise your head, and you shall bruise His heel."[8] Many Biblical scholars identify the Seed of Eve as Jesus Christ, but Biblical commentators are often reticent to speculate on the seed of the serpent.

It is clear from this point on that God had a plan to redeem mankind and restore the fellowship lost in the Fall. It is also clear that the Savior whom God intended from the beginning would be the "Seed" of woman. Satan still had (and has) considerable power.[9] So, Satan set about doing whatever he could to tempt mankind to evil and incite rebellion. Satan's ultimate goal, however, was to stop God from fulfilling His promise of sending the Seed of woman to destroy Satan and Satan's seed. It is this attempt by Satan to destroy mankind and stop the birth of the Savior that he knew would destroy him that forms the background against which the drama of the Old Testament is played out.

> Now it came to pass, when men began to multiply on the face of the earth, and daughters were born to them, that the sons of God saw the daughters of men, that they were beautiful; and they took wives for themselves of all whom they chose. And the Lord said, "My Spirit shall not strive with man forever, for he is indeed flesh; yet his days shall be one hundred and twenty years." There were giants on the earth in those days, and also afterward, when the sons of God came in to the daughters of men and they bore children to them. Those were the mighty men who were of old, men of renown. Then the Lord saw that the wickedness of man was great in the earth, and that every intent of the thoughts of his heart was only evil continually. And the Lord was sorry that He had made man on the earth, and He was grieved in His heart. So the Lord said, "I will

---

7 Genesis 3:7-10. I also strongly recommend *True Faced* by Bill Thrall, Bruce McNicol, and John Lynch on the subject of leaving behind a life of hiddenness and shame for an environment of grace.

8 Genesis 3:15

9 Greg Boyd's *Satan and the Problem of Evil* makes a detailed case for angelic free will along with human free will and the role that free will plays in sin and suffering here on earth.

> destroy man whom I have created from the face of the earth, both man and beast, creeping thing and birds of the air, for I am sorry that I have made them." But Noah found grace in the eyes of the Lord. This is the genealogy of Noah. Noah was a just man, perfect in his generations. Noah walked with God. And Noah begot three sons: Shem, Ham, and Japheth. The earth also was corrupt before God and the earth was filled with violence. So God looked upon the earth, and indeed it was corrupt; for all flesh had corrupted their way on the earth.[10]

Genesis 6 is crucial to understanding the reason for the Flood. It is not just that mankind was sinful, but that mankind itself had been corrupted by intermarriage with the "sons of God," or angels. Some of these hybrid children were giants, but all of them were apparently quite evil. This is one example where modern Bible scholars and teachers often try to explain away or ignore references to things like giants even though there is a lot of archeological evidence for giants.[11] In this wicked and corrupted environment, we find Noah, who is described as "perfect in his generations." This could very well mean that Noah was pure human with no angelic corruption of his bloodline. This is perhaps part of the reason genealogies play such a prominent role in scripture. It is this pure human bloodline from which God promised to bring a Savior whom we now know as Jesus Christ. In order to preserve this Messianic bloodline, God chose to destroy the "corrupted flesh" of the rest of mankind.

The Flood was not the end of the Nephilim, or human-angel hybrid, problem. Either through the wives of Noah's sons or through new occurrences of human and angel interbreeding, Nephilim and evil men continued to do Satan's bidding in attempting to corrupt and thereby destroy the purely human bloodline of the promised Messiah.[12] In Genesis 10:8, we find that "Cush begot Nimrod; he began to be a mighty one on the earth." Given Nimrod's infamy throughout the ancient world and the fact that he was apparently

10 Genesis 6:1-12

11 See www.stevequayle.com for pictures and documents relating to giants.

12 See the Book of Enoch (especially chapters VI—XVI) for a more detailed account of the "Watchers" who chose to disobey God and left the heavenly realm to have sexual relationships with human women and to teach men to work with metals, stone, etc.

changed during his lifetime, some Christian writers believe that Nimrod was subject to genetic alteration by angels, or "Watchers," as Enoch calls them.[13] It is certainly possible that Satan's angels were engaging in what modern scientists would call genetic alteration and manipulation of people like Nimrod in order to turn them into "mighty" and corrupt killing machines.

According to the Book of Enoch, men sought the influence and intervention of angelic forces to teach them to make better weapons, jewelry, herbal formulas, and to understand astronomy/astrology.[14] It is only when we consider angelic intervention that the incredible technological advancement of some of the ancient civilizations (Egypt with its pyramids, Babylon and its hanging gardens and flushing toilets, etc.) can be reasonably explained. While mainstream history attempts to portray everything as a steady but incremental progression of technological advancement; the opposite is found in ancient societies such as Egypt. The peak of Egyptian civilization was achieved quite quickly with the building of the Great Pyramid.[15] There has been a lot of speculative material written on the crypto-historical record of ancient civilizations, but I am not interested in delving deeply into it in this book. My assertion is simply that angelic entities played a significant role in the technological development of human civilizations.

It is a widely accepted interpretation of the Bible to consider the term "heavens" to mean an area that while invisible and seemingly inaccessible to us, is right over our heads. In this area modern physics is once again catching up to the Bible.[16] If we

13 www.peeringintodarkness.com is a website dedicated to this type of theorizing. Sue Bradley, Sharon Gilbert, Tom Horn, and Russ Dizdar (someone I highly respect) have written and discussed the possibility of genetic manipulation by angelic/demonic forces.

14 Book of Enoch chapter VIII

15 The Great Pyramid is an object of extreme interest to a variety of conspiracy researchers. It is also an object of veneration among the Freemasons and other Luciferian and occult groups. I can't say I endorse all of David Flynn's theories, but his material on the numerological significance of both the location and dimensions of the Great Pyramid is quite interesting. Flynn's website is http://www.mt.net/~watcher/

16 I enjoy the anecdote about the group of physicists who climb what they believe to be the final peak of scientific enquiry only to find that the theologians are there waiting for them.

consider modern superstring theory's prediction of a ten or eleven dimensional universe, it appears that modern science is gradually coming around to the idea of what Christians refer to as spiritual reality.[17]

It is in the context of inter-dimensional contact and communication that the account of the Tower of Babel in Genesis 11 begins to make sense. According to Genesis 11:4, man was attempting to build "a tower whose top is in the heavens." God, instead of denying the plausibility of their endeavor (as we might expect if they were simply trying to build a tower into the sky), says the following:

> Indeed the people are one and they all have one language, and this is what they begin to do; now nothing that they propose to do will be withheld from them. Come, let Us go down and there confuse their language, that they may not understand one another's speech.[18]

As with all of God's prohibitions, He is looking out for the best interest of mankind with this barrier between humanity and the heavens. Looking at how mankind usually uses the latest technology to find new ways to kill and oppress each other, it is hard to question God on this one.[19]

After the Flood and the scattering of nations through the Tower of Babel, God chose for Himself a people to specifically guard and protect. Part of God's reason for establishing the nation of Israel appears to be to have a people "set apart" and to have the human bloodline protected from angelic corruption. It is important to understand the necessity and the function of this in God's plan for the salvation of mankind. God established the law of Israel in order to keep the Israelites mindful of their own sinfulness and of their need for a Savior. Indeed, salvation for

---

17 See Brian Greene's *Elegant Universe: Superstrings, Hidden Dimensions, and the Quest for the Ultimate Theory* for a very interesting and readable description of superstring theory.

18 Genesis 11:6-7

19 Globalization is the process by which the world's elite are trying to reverse what God did at the Tower of Babel. This includes the pressuring of people all over the world to learn English in order survive in the "global economy." In fact, it is intriguing to look at the most expensive project in human history (CERN's Large Hadron Collider) as perhaps a new attempt at a Tower of Babel type project.

all mankind depended on Abraham and his descendants remaining set apart from the corrupted bloodlines of the angel/human hybrids and from the worship of false gods, angelic entities who rebelled against God and sought worship themselves.

It is with the salvation of mankind hanging in the balance that God's commands regarding the Promised Land begin to make sense to us. Once Satan found out that Canaan was to be the Promised Land, he had about 400 years to lay one giant (pun intended) minefield in the way of God's plan. Satan filled the land with Nephilim and with wicked people following after wicked gods. When we read that Joshua had everyone in places such as Hazor killed with the sword and that this was done in obedience to God's command,[20] it is tempting for us to see this as unnecessary and cruel. In fact, many have used God's instructions to the Israelites regarding Canaan as an excuse to reject God as cruel and as encouraging genocide.[21] A proper understanding of the Canaanites reveals people (including giants)[22] infected with the Nephilim bloodlines, empowered by Satan's angelic forces, and manipulated by Satan himself in Satan's attempt to destroy the human race by whom he knew God intended to bring forth the "Son of Man" who would defeat him and ultimately destroy him. As Chris White says in his video *Genocide in the Bible?*, "if you want to say 'God should have let the 13 foot tall evil hybrids bent on the destruction of humanity for the purpose of destroying any chance of the redemption of man go,' then you are free to think what you want [about God]." Obviously, I am making the argument that God was more than justified in ordering the complete destruction of certain tribes in the land of Canaan.

It is against the backdrop of spiritual warfare and Satan's plot to infect and corrupt humanity that God's prohibition on the worship of other gods takes on even greater urgency. God lovingly placed boundaries to protect not only His chosen people from sin and idolatry, but all of mankind from eternal damnation. It

20 Joshua 11:10-15

21 I highly recommend Chris White's video *Genocide in the Bible?* on this subject. Much of the argument I am presenting in this section comes from this video and from hearing Chris discuss this topic with others. Chris's YouTube channel is knowwheretorun1984. http://www.youtube.com/watch?v=vnFB3p7tmbA

22 Numbers 13:33, Deuteronomy 2:11-3:13, Joshua 12:4, 13:12, and 17:15

is modern, western prejudice, however, to presume that worshipping gods consisted merely of superstitious kneeling and sacrificing before material objects like a golden calf. These false gods were real spiritual entities with real power to influence things on the earth. Without exception, we find evidence of the worship of these false gods in every ancient civilization.

Before the Israelites could enter the Promised Land of Canaan, God had to bring them out of slavery in Egypt. This is a familiar story but there are a couple of points that I want to highlight here. God, as depicted in the Bible, is a God in conflict with Satan and with satanic world systems. This is clearly shown through the Biblical account of the life of Moses. Moses was born to a slave people but a people whom the Pharaoh feared so much that he was attempting to have a genocidal policy of killing the sons of the Hebrews enforced throughout Egypt.[23] Thanks to the Hebrew midwives' fear of God and resulting disobedience to their government, however, Moses was not killed when he was born.

Skipping forward in Moses' life, we find Moses returning to Egypt in order to be used by God to deliver his people from slavery. The signs that God instructed and empowered him to do in front of Pharaoh are clear evidence of God's power over what we perceive as natural laws. However, it is interesting to note that Pharaoh's 'wise men,' 'sorcerers,' and 'magicians' were able to imitate some of Moses and Aaron's miracles.[24] It is rightly often pointed out that God's power exceeds that of the spiritual forces behind the Egyptian sorcerers, but it is still important to note that these sorcerers possessed, or perhaps more accurately were possessed by, powers to do things not explainable by human effort alone. God's enemies have significant power to influence the natural world, but it is of course exceeded— not eliminated, by the power of God.[25]

The fallen angels and Nephilim brought ancient societies, such as the Sumerians, Babylonians, Egyptians, and Mayans,

23 Exodus 1-2

24 Exodus 4-12

25 I am not all questioning God's omnipotence. I am just trying to express the dynamics of the spiritual world as the Bible presents them. Obviously if you trace the source of power or being back far enough it always goes back to God, but the God of the Bible treats both men and angels as free beings and holds them accountable for their freely chosen actions.

incredible technological advancement and knowledge of architecture, astronomy, and weapons manufacturing. However, these advances were not free. The price was a tyrannical system of rule where the few, often considered gods themselves, ruled the many with an iron fist. Furthermore, the gods that brought the forbidden knowledge demanded bloody sacrifices in return. Human sacrifice and even cannibalism is a common thread throughout many ancient societies. These heinous activities are still practiced in secret today in satanic ritual abuse and at secretive gatherings of the political elite such as Bohemian Grove.[26] The systems of control that exhibit themselves in ancient societies and today's societies are clearly unsustainable. The corrupt, vicious, and morally bankrupt behavior that they foster (human sacrifice, pedophilia, inbreeding, etc.), lead fairly quickly to the destruction of these civilizations and empires.

The occult knowledge that the ancient civilizations received from the gods never disappeared entirely, however, even with the collapse of empires. The occult knowledge has been passed down through small groups of people all the way to the present day. This knowledge is compartmentalized and passed along in secret societies such as the Freemasons or Illuminati. This knowledge is about both the physical and spiritual world.[27] The passing of this knowledge is often accompanied by rituals which open doors to angelic and demonic influence.[28]

If we ignore the reality of spiritual warfare that has been going on since the beginning of mankind, we cannot accurately understand the world we live in today or its history. As we have seen in this chapter, God's commands to the Israelites in the Old Testament regarding Canaan make sense only in a context of a spiritual war with powerful satanic forces and a physical battle to protect the human bloodline from Nephilim infection. Israel's frequent idolatry and turning away from God makes sense only

26 I will expand and support these claims later in this book when I discuss secret societies and the occult practices of the elite.

27 For example, the Freemasons trace their building secrets back to the Egyptians.

28 There are many levels to the societies such as the Freemasons. Those on the outer level, called "porch masons," may very well have no bad intentions and not realize that the "harmless rituals" they practice are imitations and gateways into much more spiritually destructive rituals.

if we admit that the idols represented real entities and endowed real power on their worshippers.[29] When Israel was faithful to God, they were unstoppable militarily and experienced incredible blessings. When unfaithful, however, Israel was overrun and subjected to many types of slavery, oppression, and bondage.

Israel was designed by God as a theocracy executed through a clear set of laws that were enforced in clearly delineated ways. Importantly, it was designed as a system where the laws applied to everyone in the society. No man was above the law or had the authority to change the law according to his whims. A key event in Israel's history occurred when the people demanded a king. God knew this was a bad idea, of course, but chose to grant their request.

> Now it came to pass when Samuel was old that he made his sons judges over Israel. The name of his firstborn was Joel, and the name of his second, Abijah; *they were* judges in Beersheba. But his sons did not walk in his ways; they turned aside after dishonest gain, took bribes, and perverted justice. Then all the elders of Israel gathered together and came to Samuel at Ramah, and said to him, "Look, you are old, and your sons do not walk in your ways. Now make us a king to judge us like all the nations." But the thing displeased Samuel when they said, "Give us a king to judge us." So Samuel prayed to the LORD. And the LORD said to Samuel, "Heed the voice of the people in all that they say to you; for they have not rejected you, but they have rejected Me, that I should not reign over them. According to all the works which they have done since the day that I brought them up out of Egypt, even to this day—with which they have forsaken Me and served other gods—so they are doing to you also. Now therefore, heed their voice. However, you shall solemnly forewarn them, and show them the behavior of the king who will reign over them." So Samuel told all the words of the LORD to the people who asked him for a king. And he said, "This will be the behavior of the king who will reign over you: He will take your sons and appoint *them* for his own chariots and *to be* his horsemen, and *some* will run before his chariots. He will appoint captains over his fifties, *will set some* to plow his ground and reap his harvest, and *some* to make his weapons of war and equipment for his chariots. He will take your daughters *to be* perfumers, cooks,

29 Lesser power than offered by God, of course, but still tempting because of Satan's appeal to our prideful and rebellious sin nature.

> and bakers. And he will take the best of your fields, your vineyards, and your olive groves, and give *them* to his servants. He will take a tenth of your grain and your vintage, and give it to his officers and servants. And he will take your male servants, your female servants, your finest young men, and your donkeys, and put *them* to his work. He will take a tenth of your sheep. And you will be his servants. And you will cry out in that day because of your king whom you have chosen for yourselves, and the LORD will not hear you in that day."
>
> Nevertheless the people refused to obey the voice of Samuel; and they said, "No, but we will have a king over us, that we also may be like all the nations, and that our king may judge us and go out before us and fight our battles."[30]

This passage is crucial to understanding the role of political power both in Israel and in all nations. God makes it clear in this passage that it is His rule that the people are rejecting. God also makes it clear that having a king will mean hardship for the people. This is not only true with "bad kings," or "bad governments," it is true with all governments where men wield political power over other men. Up until this point, Israel was a theocracy governed under the rule of law. This system did not function perfectly because God still allowed judges to make decisions and some of the judges, such as Samuel's sons, were corrupt.

However, God makes it clear in this passage that corruption within the system of a rule of law is far less intrusive and damaging to the people than to be subject to the rule of men. Much pain and suffering came out of this decision for the Israelites. Furthermore, much pain and suffering has been the result of rule by men throughout history. Satan is the driving force behind political power, the power to bend another's will into submission to your own through force or the threat of force. That is why God occasionally upsets the "natural" worldly order of things to show that He is ultimately in control and that one day the tyranny will end.

We can see the contrast between the worldly satanic system of power, and God's Kingdom, by looking at Saul and David. Saul was a "mighty man of power"[31] and tall and handsome to boot. This was exactly the type of king the people wanted and God

30 I Samuel 8:1-20

31 I Samuel 9:1

granted their wish. This did not work out well for Israel. Saul was quickly corrupted by his new power and proceeded to lead the Israelites ever farther from following the will of God. Saul even performed unlawful sacrifices,[32] refused to kill Agag when God ordered him to do so,[33] and consulted a medium.[34]

David, on the other hand, was an unlikely king by the world's standards. His family was far from powerful, he was the youngest son, and he was not physically intimidating. But, David was a man after God's own heart.[35] God loves to work through unlikely heroes in nearly impossible situations so that we can know that the power comes from God and not ourselves. David learned to trust and rely on God through encounters with fierce enemies that included a lion, the giant Goliath, and King Saul. David was rewarded by God's promise that his line would endure and that the Messiah would come from his descendants.[36]

Even David, however, was corrupted by the power of his office and caused the people of Israel to suffer under his reign. While some of this suffering was indirectly related to David's kingship, his sinful decisions led to the death and destruction of many of his people. Uriah was placed on the front lines to be killed so David could cover up his adultery with Bathsheba.[37] David ordered a census of his people which showed that he was beginning to trust the strength of his military instead of God alone.[38] Some scholars believe that David was considering instituting a military draft to form a standing army.[39] While David realized the sinfulness of his decision soon after the census was tallied, the people had to pay a steep price. 70,000 men died because of the three day plague inflicted on the people because of David's decision to take a census.

---

32 I Samuel 13
33 I Samuel 15:1-9
34 I Samuel 28:3-25
35 I Samuel 13:14
36 II Samuel 7:12-16
37 II Samuel 11
38 II Samuel 24
39 A footnote in the NKJV Nelson Study Bible for II Samuel 24:3 states "this census was the first step in preparing for a military draft. God's plan seems to have been for Israel to have a citizen army rather than a large standing army, so that Israel would trust in His protection."

The book of Job is one of the oldest books in the Bible. But, its theological lessons are still quite relevant for us today. One of the major themes in Job is the cause of human suffering, which is still an important topic to any thinking person today. Job also gives us some insight into the way things work in the spiritual realm and the dynamic between God, Satan, angelic forces, and mankind.

In the first chapter of Job we get a behind the scenes look into the order of the spiritual aspects of the universe.

> Now there was a day when the sons of God came to present themselves before the LORD, and Satan also came among them. And the LORD said to Satan, "From where do you come?"
>
> So Satan answered the LORD and said, "From going to and fro on the earth, and from walking back and forth on it."
>
> Then the LORD said to Satan, "Have you considered My servant Job, that *there is* none like him on the earth, a blameless and upright man, one who fears God and shuns evil?"
>
> So Satan answered the LORD and said, "Does Job fear God for nothing? Have You not made a hedge around him, around his household, and around all that he has on every side? You have blessed the work of his hands, and his possessions have increased in the land. But now, stretch out Your hand and touch all that he has, and he will surely curse You to Your face!"
>
> And the Lord said to Satan, "Behold, all that he has *is* in your power; only do not lay a hand on his *person.*"[40]

There are a number of interesting observations to glean from this passage. First and foremost, it is clear that Satan, or the Adversary of God, is on the same level as the other "sons of God," or angels, and that he is still subject to the authority of God. Second, it is clear that Satan spends at least some of his time going "to and fro" on the earth seeking to wreak havoc and destruction.[41] Third, we can infer from the passage that Satan had already attempted to harm Job and his family but that God had placed a protective "hedge" around him and his household that Satan could not penetrate. Finally, we see that Satan is confident that

40 Job 1:6-12

41 I Peter 5:8 "Be sober, be vigilant; because your adversary the devil walks about like a roaring lion, seeking whom he may devour."

Job's allegiance to God is based on his circumstances, not on his love and obedience to God Himself.

The rest of the book proves Satan wrong. No matter how bad Job's circumstances get he refuses to curse God even though he believes he has been treated unfairly by God. This reveals a few more important things about Satan, the Adversary of God and His people. Satan is finite and limited. While he may be more brilliant than any man and has the advantage of thousands of years of experience observing and attempting to manipulate human behavior, he is unable to accurately predict Job's response to the terrible circumstances Satan puts him through. He is also unable to read Job's mind/heart in the first place to see where his motivation for obedience comes from.

We can also learn important things about God from the book of Job. We see that He is proud of His obedient children, even going so far as to brag about Job to Satan. We see that God is sovereign over all things, including Satan, but that He grants freedom within limits He determines. We see that God knows the heart of Job and knew that Job's obedience to Him was not based on blessed circumstances but on true love and obedience.

The majority of the chapters of Job consist of Job's "friends" telling him to repent and that God is punishing him for his sinfulness. While Job's friends rightfully get a bad rap from modern readers, their statements were considered theologically accurate during Job's time and are still the same assumptions believed and preached in many churches today (i.e. good circumstances are a sign of God's blessing, bad circumstances are God's punishment for sin). Job's complaints, on the other hand, were also not accurate. He believed God was punishing him incorrectly or too harshly for sins that he did not commit or that God was somehow absent or unaware of what was happening.[42] Satan, Job, his friends, his wife, Elihu—all of them had an incomplete and inaccurate view of what was really going on, and of why those terrible things were happening to Job.

It is only when God replies to Job's complaints with a few questions of His own that Job gets an accurate understanding of God and His works.[43] God makes Job aware that He is dealing

42 Job 19:23-29, 21:7-21
43 Job 40-41

with forces of chaos called behemoth and Leviathan that Job is no match for and does not understand. This is perhaps the most important lesson from the book of Job. When we or those we love are afflicted with horrific and seemingly random suffering, we must recognize that we do not know the whole story. While some bad circumstances may be God's punishment for sin and designed to induce repentance, not all suffering falls into this category. Ultimately, God is sovereign and just. But, during this finite time period we must understand that there are many forces at work in the universe that God allows and sets limits on but that are not directly controlled by His will. Satan has power only in the realm of our circumstances. He cannot destroy our souls. When we develop a mindset that is focused on the Kingdom of God instead of the kingdoms of this world, we will "not fear those who kill the body but cannot kill the soul."[44]

44 Matthew 10:28

## Chapter 3

# Good and Evil: The Battle from the Time of Christ to Modernity

Jesus Christ's birth, death, and resurrection changed the course of not only human history, but also the course of the entire physical and spiritual universe. It is interesting that there is a gap of 400 years between the events of the Old Testament and the events in the New Testament. We could even say that God was "quiet" during those years. Perhaps part of the reason for this is that God did not want to tip His hand, so to speak, to Satan. Satan knew that his ultimate defeat would come at the hands of a Messiah born of the descendants of King David. It is important to remember that Satan, unlike God, is not omniscient or omnipresent. What Satan did have working to his advantage was influence over the rulers of the worldly kingdoms. One of these rulers was Herod the Great.

In Matthew Chapter Two, we read that when Herod found out from the wise men from the East that the King of the Jews had been born, he tried to get them to come back and tell him exactly where the young Jesus was. When God intervened through his loyal angels to warn the wise men not to return to Herod, Herod responded by ordering the slaughter of all young males in the area. Herod here exhibits the fruit of satanic political power: fear of losing control and utter lack of concern for human life. Imagine the level of tyranny necessary for a ruler to be able to have an order carried out to murder all young males in a whole city and surrounding area. God responds by warning Joseph to flee into Egypt. It is very possible that at this point Satan still does not know that Jesus is the Messiah. It is even possible that Satan expected (like much of the Jewish religious establishment), that Jesus would appear as a political leader in order to take away Satan's power through his political minions.

It is interesting that in Luke we find John's baptism of Jesus followed directly by the genealogy of Jesus Christ.[1] This is important because God, through Luke, is verifying that Jesus Christ is of an uncorrupted bloodline and is the Son of Man that He promised in the Garden of Eden after the Fall of man. Satan's plan to prevent the birth of the Messiah through the corruption of the genetics of mankind had failed. Next, Luke records Satan's attempt to tempt Jesus Christ to sin in the wilderness.

> Then the devil, taking Him up on a high mountain, showed Him all the kingdoms of the world in a moment of time. And the devil said to Him, "All this authority I will give You, and their glory; for *this* has been delivered to me, and I give it to whomever I wish. Therefore, if You will worship before me, all will be Yours."
>
> And Jesus answered and said to him, "Get behind Me, Satan! For it is written, '*You shall worship the LORD your God, and Him only you shall serve.*'"[2]

This particular temptation (one of many that occurred during the 40 days), and Jesus' response, is crucial to understanding the way the kingdoms of this world operate.

Satan offers Jesus authority over the kingdoms of the earth. Satan further asserts that "I give it to whomever I wish." This authority is offered conditionally, however, on Jesus worshipping Satan. Is it possible that this deal has been offered to prospective kings, dictators, presidents, and other wielders of political power throughout history? While I am not claiming that today's world leaders are literally taken to a mountain top by the devil himself, it is hard to deny that there is some connection between the Luciferian religion that is prevalent among the world's elite and Satan's limited authority to grant political kingdoms.

The occult obsession of many of the world's elite is not well known but is easily provable with a little bit of research. For example, Tony Blair has admitted to making political decisions after communing with a force that he calls "The Light."[3] Another example is leaders including George W. Bush, George H.W. Bush,

---

1 Luke 3

2 Luke 4:5-8

3 "Blair revelations reiterate elite occult obsession" by Steve Watson. http://www.prisonplanet.com/Pages/Sept05/210905Blair_revelations.htm

Henry Kissinger, Colin Powell, Arnold Schwarzenegger, Richard Nixon, and Ronald Reagan attending the annual secret meetings of the Bohemian Club in the Bohemian Grove in California. This is where "conservative" leaders get together to participate in homosexual activities along with idol worship and "mock" human sacrifice.[4] The relationship of the occult and political power will be explored more throughout this book, but what I want to emphasize here is the connection which Satan claims between political power and worship of Satan.

Of course, Satan's authority to grant control of kingdoms is limited and is (as even he admits) "delivered to [him]" by God. This authority is for a finite time and is surely restrained by other limits that God has put in place as well. That being said, the events of history become much clearer when we look for the hand of Satan pulling the strings of world rulers and not the hand of God alone.[5]

Jesus refuses the temptation of political power even more forcefully than he rejects the other two temptations recorded in this encounter. Jesus knew how much good He could accomplish if He was in control of the kingdoms of this world. He also knew that taking this route would allow Him to avoid the physical, emotional, and spiritual suffering of the cross and the cup of God's wrath. Most importantly, however, He knew that worship of Satan would separate Him from God forever and would doom all of mankind to damnation.

It is revealing that Satan sought Jesus' worship, because it is the desire for worship that inspired Satan to rebel in the first place.[6] While Satan has sought and received the worship of many powerful men throughout history, the worship of Jesus Christ went to God alone. Sin is not fulfilling, even for Satan himself. No matter how much power he wields, no matter how many lives he crushes, ruins, and destroys, he will never be satisfied. Satan

---

4 I highly recommend the Alex Jones documentary *Dark Secrets: Inside Bohemian Grove*. It is available (as with all of Alex's fine documentaries) for free on the internet. http://video.google.com/videoplay? docid=5688492591288248198

5 For a detailed discussion of the theological basis for this outlook, I highly recommend *Satan and the Problem of Evil: Constructing a Trinitarian Warfare Theodicy* by Gregory A. Boyd.

6 See Isaiah 14:12-21 for the account of Lucifer's rebellion and what the ultimate outcome of his rebellion will be for him and his followers.

will always be jealous of God and of Jesus Christ. This same disease is also characteristic of Satan's minions in the New World Order. No matter how much power they have, they want more. No matter how many lives they destroy and exploit for their own gratification they are still left craving more and more until the day of their destruction.

Instead of seizing the thrones of this world through bended knee to Satan, Jesus Christ earned the right to rule upon the throne at God's right hand through enduring the agony of God's wrath and conquering the power of death. Throughout Christ's ministry, He focused on the idea that He was bringing the Kingdom of God to earth and that because of Him we are able to experience the Kingdom of God and bring it to others.[7]

What does this mean? What is the Kingdom of God? It is clear from Jesus' teachings that the Kingdom of God is not "of this world" and cannot be brought about by worldly means.[8] The Kingdom of God is the antithesis of the satanic kingdoms of this world. Jesus teaches that the Kingdom of God belongs to the poor and is extremely difficult for the wealthy and powerful to enter into.[9] Instead of celebrating domination and power and wicked cunning like the kingdoms of this world, entering the Kingdom of God requires becoming a servant to others and learning to trust like a child.[10] The cross of Calvary is the perfect expression of both the kingdoms of this world (forcefully inflicting suffering and death to maintain control), and the Kingdom of God (Jesus willingly sacrificing His own life and enduring God's eternal wrath so that we may live and be blameless before God).

The hallmark of the satanic kingdoms of this world is a pyramidal hierarchical structure with each level of the pyramid groveling before the level above and dominating the level below. These systems are ripe for satanic manipulation because Satan only needs to corrupt and guide the top levels of the pyramid directly and the entire system is infected with satanic influence. Conversely, Jesus Christ revealed that the Kingdom of God is realized when we allow the love and power of God to sup-

7 Matthew 12:28, Luke 4:43, Luke 9:2, Luke 9:60, etc.
8 John 18:36
9 Mark 10:23-25, Matthew 5:3.
10 Mark 9:33-37

port us and guide us as we love and serve each other. The early church met in small groups in each other's homes (or even in places like the catacombs in times of extreme persecution). The church leadership structure described in the New Testament is a brilliant plan to diffuse and decentralize power and to avoid the pyramidal structure that is so easily and so often corrupted by Satan. This structure was also quite resistant to persecution by the state.

Do our modern churches resemble the manifestation of the Kingdom of God as in the early church or do they structurally resemble the kingdoms of this world? If we structure our churches like businesses, with a pastor as powerful but often short-tenured CEO and elders functioning as a board of directors, what kingdom model are we following? If our churches are structured into a seemingly endless bureaucracy of successive levels of hierarchy, are we sure that God is at the top of the pyramid? It is important to separate churches as we think of them today from the church (the Bride of Christ) that is and always will be wholly dedicated to Jesus Christ.[11] If we are not living with the same level of commitment to Christ and to each other that was exhibited by the early church as recorded in the New Testament, then something is very, very wrong. To figure out what went wrong, we must examine the early history of the church.

Before Christ and for some time afterwards, false gods were worshipped openly. The problem for Satan and his fellow false gods was that Jesus came in and started casting out demons and exerting clear power and authority over the false gods.[12] In the gospels, disease and demonic possession are some of the chief targets of Jesus' ministry.[13] Disease is treated in the same way as demonic possession by Jesus: as a product of a fallen world and of the satanic kingdoms of this world and as something to be fought against. Jesus' disciples were also given authority over disease and demonic possession.[14] Christians in the early church continued to heal the sick and cast out demons through the power and

11 See "Paul Washer to Professing Christians" for more on this topic http://www.youtube.com/watch? v=uVlCuy3ihEo&feature=related

12 Matthew 12:28, Mark 1:34, and many others.

13 Mark 1:32-34

14 Mark 3:13-15

name of Jesus Christ.[15] This, in part, explains the exponential growth of the early church.

Satan had to do something to stop the spread of Christianity. The temptations with which he wooed worshippers to the temples of the false gods—prostitution, debauchery, etc—were beginning to lose ground to the real power, the real love, the real acceptance, and the real salvation offered by God through the death and resurrection of Christ Jesus. Satan, as Satan is wont to do, attacked Christians with the power of the state. Christianity was made illegal. Christians were impaled on poles, set on fire, fed to lions, mocked, ridiculed, starved, stripped of money and social status, thrown in jail, stoned to death, and subjected to every means of oppression and torture that the satanic minions of the Roman government and Jewish religious establishment could devise.[16] Through everything that Nero and every other tyrant could devise, however, Christianity flourished and continued expanding.

Along with oppression through powers of the worldly kingdoms, Satan attacked the teachings of the church by sending in imposters, dividers, and twisters of the gospel. His infiltrators urged compromise between trust in Jesus for salvation and reliance on Mosaic Law. They urged the combination of the gospel with the "intelligent" Gnostics. Satan did whatever he could do to distract from, alter, and water down the teaching of the coming of the Kingdom of God through Jesus Christ crucified and resurrected. These tactics by Satan and his minions did have some significant negative effects as seen by the many letters written to combat and refute the false teaching that was going on in various places. As with all things that Satan, fallen angels, and fallen men intend for evil, God redemptively used these false teachings to inspire the sound doctrine in refutation of them that is still available to us today in the form of the New Testament.

The gospel itself is terribly and fiercely simple. We cannot attain salvation or reconciliation with God through any human means. We can only receive salvation through the grace of God alone. There is no secret knowledge, no gnosis, and no path to enlighten-

15 Acts 5:12-16

16 Along with the record of these events in scripture, Fox's Book of Martyrs is a good source and is available to read online. http://www.ccel.org/f/foxe/martyrs/home.html

ment that we can feel proud of ourselves for understanding. We cannot even create the desire for repentance in our own hearts; it is the work of the Holy Spirit. God can bring even small children to an understanding of their need for Jesus. While we must become humble and broken to accept the gift of salvation from God, we do not even get to perform some self-flagellating ceremony of human striving to humble and break ourselves. We must rely instead on the Holy Spirit to intercede for us and to reveal to us our sin and desperate need for a Savior. We cannot buy God off with sacrifices, riches, or good works. We can only accept the sacrifice of Jesus Christ and the spiritual riches of knowing God that come with it.

After several hundred years of the early church, Satan was desperate for a new strategy. He found that he could not destroy the church with the state so he decided to merge the state and the church in order to corrupt Christianity with the poison of political power. With Constantine's supposed vision[17]—either made up by him in a politically savvy move, or brought about by satanic spiritual forces—Satan set about doing more damage to Christianity through Constantine than Nero could have ever dreamed of doing.

The church went from being a rag-tag group of often-persecuted Jesus followers to a major political force. As is always the case with the gain of political power, corruption was soon to follow. Christianity was merged not only with the Roman state but also with the pagan Roman sun-cult religions. This infection of false-ideology and occult beliefs wreaked havoc on the church. The accusations that many modern truth-seekers, atheists, and others fling towards Christianity today is really rooted in this hybridization of Christian teaching mixed with ancient sun-cults and political expediency. The monster that arose, the Catholic Church, went so far as to execute as heretics those who would not worship Mary (a pseudo-Christian version of occult goddess worship), or who denied other "orthodox" doctrines of the Catholic Church.[18]

---

17 Constantine reportedly looked up at the sun and saw a cross with the words "by this, conquer!" before the Battle of Milvian Bridge in 312. It is interesting that the supposed cross of his vision was in front of the sun, which is of course an object and symbol of worship in sun cults throughout history.

18 Fox's Book of Martyrs, Chapter IV http://bible.christiansunite.com/fox/fox004.shtml

This sun-cult hybridization is the reason why Christmas and Easter are celebrated on their respective dates (and for the origin of the name Easter).[19] Was it pagan religions becoming Christian or Christianity becoming paganized? Regardless, many modern criticisms, especially of the "Jesus is a myth" ilk,[20] are centered on the idea that the Roman Catholic Church represents true Christianity. An organization cannot wield political power and mimic Christ at the same time; the two are antithetical. Jesus said, "You cannot serve both God and mammon."[21] Mammon is wealth, money, or property, the basic enticements and tools of the satanic kingdoms of this world. The Roman Catholic Church stopped acting like Jesus and started acting like a tyrannical government. So, the horrors of the Crusades, Inquisition, and general oppression of people naturally followed.

The Roman Catholic Church, as with all political institutions, reacted violently whenever any actions were taken that weakened the authority of the Church. Thomas Wycliffe, for example, was hated by the Pope for his translation of the Latin Vulgate into English. Forty-four years after his death, Wycliffe's bones were dug up, crushed, and thrown in a river at the Pope's request.[22] Wycliffe planted a seed that would eventually bear fruit, although not without much more suffering being inflicted by the Roman Catholic Church.

> One of Wycliffe's followers, John Hus, actively promoted Wycliffe's ideas: that people should be permitted to read the Bible in their own language, and they should oppose the tyranny of the Roman church that threatened anyone possessing a non-Latin Bible with execution. Hus was burned at the stake in **1415**, with Wycliffe's manuscript Bibles used as kindling for the fire.[23]

---

19 "Where did "Easter" get its name?" is an excellent article on ChristianAnswers.net. http://www.christiananswers.net/q-eden/edn-t020.html The date of December 25th for the celebration of the Christ Mass, or Christmas, was decreed in 350a.d. by Pope Julius I. It was formerly the celebration of the son of Isis, part of the pagan festival for the winter solstice. "Christmas' Pagan Origins." http://www.essortment.com/all/christmaspagan_rece.htm

20 More on this subject in the chapter on the Truth Movement. I also highly recommend "Zeitgeist Refuted Final Cut" by Elliott Nesch. Available at http://www.youtube.com/watch?v=GYNmFQkHBaE

21 Matthew 6:24

22 "English Bible History" http://www.greatsite.com/timeline-english-bible-history/

23 Ibid

People reading the Bible in their native language was a threat to the Roman Catholic Church for the same reason it is a threat to any kingdom of the world system: because the Bible teaches us how to live in the Kingdom of God. Just as early Christians chose to die rather than worship Caesar or deny that Jesus Christ is God, authoritarian political systems, whether secular or religious, must keep the truth of the gospel out of the hearts and minds of men. "You shall know the truth, and the truth shall make you free."[24] Free people are always the enemy of those seeking political power. True freedom is found only through full submission to God and Christ Jesus.

Improved English translations directly from the original languages of the Bible and the means of distributing them, thanks to the invention of the printing press, made the Protestant Reformation possible. The Protestant Reformation made some excellent steps in the right direction back toward Biblical Christianity. However, while the Reformation led to church denominations that are more varied than the monolithic pyramid of the Roman Catholic Church, the pyramidal structure of church organization was unfortunately left in place. If we look at church structure in the New Testament[25] and look at our modern churches, there is little resemblance. While many decry the hundreds of splintered denominations in the modern protestant and evangelical church, very few, although the number is growing,[26] are seeking to change the architecture of churches themselves that leaves them open to Satan's attacks.

If the church, locally and as denominations and associations, wields and seeks to wield political power, it will fail in its calling to imitate Christ and bring about the Kingdom of God. Christians are called to accept the love of Jesus Christ and share that love with others by serving them. Horrors always follow when the church tries to legislate morality by supporting a pawn of Satan's system. For example, just look at the Bush presidency,[27] which was made possible by the support of evangelical Christians. Our aim must be

24 John 8:32

25 I and II Timothy are excellent resources on this subject.

26 The house church movement as well as brick and mortar churches encouraging small groups are two good examples.

27 Over 1 million Iraqi civilians dead, lies on a host of issues, etc.

to be Christ to the world, not to force non-Christians to act morally by supporting murderous and lying politicians who pay only the slightest lip service to Christianity.[28]

It is also important to realize that the worship of false gods also lost some of its "purity" during the reign of the pseudo-Christian Roman Catholic Church. The occult teachings, rituals, festivals, and all that went with them never totally disappeared. But, they were forced underground or to disguise themselves to a large extent. In Western societies, these occult teachings were kept alive by secret societies. It is no coincidence that the trademark of these secret societies is deception and an unquenchable, though often stealthy, lust for power. These occult groups place high importance on symbols, numerology, and architecture.[29] There are many things in the design of cathedrals, Masonic lodges, federal buildings, monuments, courthouses, and corporate logos that make sense only when one considers the influence of Lucifer worshipping occultists.

The power of Satan is no match for the power of Jesus Christ in an open battle. Satan learned from watching demon after demon cast out in the name of Jesus by early Christians that spiritually aware Christians empowered by the Holy Spirit posed a serious threat to his rule on this earth. Satan has the power to kill only the body. He cannot touch the soul.[30]

> When He [Jesus Christ] opened the fifth seal, I saw under the altar the souls of those who had been slain for the word of God and for the testimony which they held. And they cried with a loud voice, saying, "How long, O Lord, holy and true, until You judge and avenge our blood on those who dwell on the earth?" Then a white robe was given to each of them; and it was said to them that they should rest a little while longer, until both *the number* of their fellow servants and their brethren, who would be killed as they *were*, was completed.[31]

---

28 *Family of Secrets,* by Russ Baker, exposes the fact that George W. Bush adopted the persona of a born- again Christian because of the advice of a political strategist.

29 I highly recommend all of Chris Pinto's documentary films, but *Riddles in Stone* specifically addresses this topic. Texe Marrs also has two books: *Codex Magica* and *Mysterious Monuments* that show hundreds of examples of occult architecture and symbols as well as discussions of who is behind them and their purpose.

30 Matthew 10:28

31 Revelation 6:9-11

This passage from Revelation shows that Satan may operate under the knowledge that when a large, but finite, number of Christian Martyrs has been reached, Jesus Christ will avenge the blood of His saints. Therefore, Satan does not always seek the immediate death of Christians—an enjoyable but not particularly effective strategy from his perspective. But, instead, he often seeks to neutralize them. In most of the western world we have been fairly effectively neutralized.

When we spend most of our time watching TV and serving as nothing more than entertainment sponges, we are neutralized. When we care only about ourselves and our own health and well-being while ignoring the suffering of our neighbor, we are neutralized. When we make token protestation at the killing of 50 million babies through abortion in America but support the slaughter of millions through warfare, economic sanctions, and engineered scarcity, we are neutralized. When we spend much of our time feeling depressed and reading quasi-Christian self-help books or obsessing over our latest attempts at sin-management, we are neutralized. When we think it's cute and funny to let our children be exposed to sorcery-lite in popular children's books without discussing with them the realities of spiritual warfare, we are neutralized. And when we say we are Christians because we prayed a prayer one time in church, but we lead the same lifestyles and have the same priorities as mainstream America, we are neutralized.

As Christians, we must realize that we are in the midst of a spiritual war. Our weapons in this war include prayer, love that puts the needs of others before our own, a thirst for truth and justice for the oppressed and persecuted people of this world, and faith that we really, truly, utterly, can trust God.

God's will is not hard to figure out. God loves mankind, He hates sin and He hates disease, suffering, and death. He loves truth, justice, mercy, and He loves to shower grace on those of us who least deserve it. The world around you and your place in it will make sense when you realize we live in a war zone, not a God puppet show. Satan and his minions have real power to affect the quality and length of our lives on this planet for the time-being. Even here on Satan's home turf, however, God is constantly redeeming pain, suffering, and even sinful actions and their consequences for His glory and our benefit.[32] But, we must learn that God is not the source of pain and suffering. In a universe composed solely of God and beings doing the will of God there would be no sin. There would be no pain. There would be no suffering. There would be no death. We do not live in that universe, yet. Thus, Jesus prayed for God's will to be done on earth as it is in heaven.[33] Now, let us examine the machinations and mechanisms of the kingdoms of this fallen world.

32 By benefit I do not mean circumstances that are better. Our true well-being has little to nothing to do with our circumstances and God often uses the worst of times to show us that He alone meets our true and deepest needs.

33 Matthew 6:8-13 The model prayer that Jesus revealed to his disciples clearly shows the disconnect between the Kingdom of God where God's name is hallowed and His will is done and the state of the kingdoms of this world where God's name is profaned and His will is not done.

## Chapter 4

# The Banks and the Real Bank Robbers: The Easiest Way to Rob a Bank is to Own All of Them

> There were also *some* who said, "We have mortgaged our lands and vineyards and houses, that we might buy grain because of the famine.
>
> There were also those who said, "We have borrowed money for the king's tax *on* our lands and vineyards. Yet now our flesh *is* as the flesh of our brethren, our children as their children; and indeed we are forcing our sons and our daughters to be slaves, and *some* of our daughters have been brought into slavery. It *is* not in our power *to redeem them*, for other men have our lands and vineyards."
>
> And I became very angry when I heard their outcry and these words. After serious thought, I rebuked the nobles and rulers, and said to them, "Each of you is exacting usury from his brother." So I called a great assembly against them.[1]

The above passage from Nehemiah demonstrates that oppression through usury, taxation, and control of mortgaged property is nothing new. Our banking and mortgage systems today are in some ways less advanced. And, in every way more oppressive, than the system the Israelites were to follow under God's Law. Specifically, God ordered that every fifty years would be a Year of Jubilee and that all debts would be forgiven and all property returned to the family of the original owner.[2] This prevented vast accumulation of wealth and property into the hands of a few and guaranteed a reasonable expectation of property ownership for large numbers of people.

1 Nehemiah 5:3-7

2 Leviticus 25:10

The financial system is the key to the New World Order's power in the material world. This chapter includes a brief history of fractional-reserve banking, the history and role of central banks in the world economy, and the ignominious history and role of America's latest central bank, the Federal Reserve. In addition, we will explore the future of this system and the role of a Bank of the World that the New World Order is attempting to set up.

Usury and money manipulation is nothing new, of course. Jesus Christ's only use of force in his ministry was when he overturned the money changers' tables in the temple and chased them out.[3] Their scam was to corner the market on silver half-shekels—the only acceptable currency for sacrifice in the temple because it did not bear the image of a pagan ruler and consistently contained the same amount of silver. The money changers then charged exorbitant rates to all visitors to the temple seeking to exchange their currency.[4] This manipulation of a prized commodity is child's play in comparison with the modern scam of fractional reserve banking.

The practice of fractional reserve banking can be traced back to goldsmiths in medieval Europe. These goldsmiths began issuing paper receipts and charging a fee for the service of keeping clients' gold locked safely away in their vaults. These receipts were then exchanged as a type of currency because it was easier and safer than lugging around a bunch of gold. What the goldsmiths figured out, however, was that only a small number of people ever came in at the same time to redeem their receipts for actual gold. So, the goldsmiths would invest much of the gold they were supposed to be holding because they rarely had to produce large amounts of it. This led to them gaining enough wealth and power to drastically affect the economy although they would occasionally get chased out of the country when their scams were discovered.[5]

Another trick developed during this time period was the coordinated expansion and contraction of the money supply.

---

3 Mark 11:15-19

4 *The Money Masters: How International Bankers Gained Control of America* –I cannot recommend this film strongly enough. It is well presented, thoroughly documented, and will give you an excellent understanding of the financial system just by taking the three and a half hours to watch it. Bill Still and Pat Carmack are responsible for this film and you can find out more at www.themoneymasters.com

5 Ibid

Loans, collateralized by real estate or other property, were given freely for a period of time. This resulted in inflation and rapid growth of the economy. As with all periods of artificial monetary expansion, these periods were rife with mal-investment because it was easy to make a profit. It was easy because everyone had plenty of money and even if a venture wasn't profitable more loans were readily available to cover losses. This expansion, or monetary inflation, was then ended in a co-ordinated way and the money supply was contracted. This resulted in a certain percentage of loan defaults, which meant the goldsmiths could seize real property from former borrowers for no reason except for the issuance of paper receipts that were backed by a tiny fraction of the value of the paper loan. This deliberate expansion and contraction of the monetary supply as a means of wealth consolidation is now taught in fraudulent schools of economics as the business cycle.[6]

Fractional reserve banking was not allowed to develop unopposed however. King Henry the First introduced the tally stick system which was an interest free fiat money system. Tally sticks were accepted because Henry accepted them for the payment of taxes. This created a market for them and made them valuable for exchanges between private parties as well. This system competed well with gold and silver coins that were also used as currency. The tally stick system lasted for 754 years and is to date the longest lasting fiat system that has been devised.[7]

The heirs to the money changers and goldsmiths were the bankers, in particular the Rothschild family. The Bank of England was established in 1694 because a desperate British government was fighting several wars for which it could not pay. The deceptively named Bank of England—really a private group of bank shareholders—was given the power to create money out of nothing and loan it to the British Empire at interest. This loan was guaranteed and collateralized by the promise that the British subjects would be responsible for paying it back through taxes on

6 Ibid

7 "The History of Money" http://www.scribd.com/doc/7505858/The-History-of-Money This is an excellent resource. If you read this document and watch The Money Masters, you will have a much clearer understanding of monetary history.

their income. To summarize, the Bank of England creates money out of nothing, loans it to a government to pay for wars it cannot otherwise afford, and then collects interest on the loans which are paid by tax-paying citizens.

The Rothschild family took central banking and fractional reserve banking to new levels. By specializing in war profiteering and loaning money to both sides in virtually every war, the Rothschilds took advantage of an advanced private intelligence network to become the richest family in the world. One example of the means for the building of the Rothschild's empire was the chicanery of Nathan Rothschild in London during the Battle of Waterloo. Rothschild was informed by his intelligence agent that Napoleon had been defeated. He then began to sell his holdings, giving the impression that Napoleon had won. This incited a massive sell-off of stocks. Simultaneously, Rothschild had his agents buy up stocks at pennies on the dollar. By the time the truth about Waterloo arrived, Nathan Rothschild had purchased most of London.[8]

As Gerald Celente points out in Alex Jones's film, *The Obama Deception*, American history is replete with examples of the bankers trying to impose a central bank and various leaders (Andrew Jackson, Abraham Lincoln, John F. Kennedy, etc.) attempting to fight them off.[9] The Federal Reserve was not the first central bank in America's history but it has been the longest lasting and most devastating. As we explore the history and machinations of the Federal Reserve, remember that "the borrower is servant to the lender."[10]

The Federal Reserve is often mentioned in the corporate media but its actions are little understood by the general public. First, it is important to realize that the Federal Reserve is not Federal and has little if any financial reserves. "The Federal Reserve is as federal as Federal Express," as Dennis Kucinich said on the floor of the House of Representatives.[11] The name was chosen, just as "Bank of England" or the first American central

8 *The Money Masters*

9 I highly recommend *The Obama Deception* as a great introduction to the actual political system in the western world. http://www.youtube.com/watch?v=eAaQNACwaLw&feature=fvst

10 Proverbs 22:7

11 This quote is featured in *The Obama Deception* and is also easily findable on YouTube.

bank—the "Bank of the United States," to give the impression of being part of the government and working for the best interest of the American people. The immense power of the Federal Reserve and all central banks rests in the power of money creation and the ability to expand and contract the money supply at will.

> Banking was conceived in iniquity and was born in sin. The bankers own the earth. Take it away from them, but leave them the power to create money, and with the flick of the pen they will create enough deposits to buy it back again. However, take it away from them, and all the great fortunes like mine will disappear and they ought to disappear, for this would be a happier and better world to live in. But, if you wish to remain the slaves of bankers and pay the cost of your own slavery, let them continue to create money.[12]

With the Federal Reserve Act of 1913, Congress turned its constitutionally designated authority to create and regulate money over to a private corporation of big bankers.[13]

Now that Congress had forfeited the ability to create money interest free, they needed a way to pay interest on the money the government was now forced to borrow.[14] This money was provided via the new federal income tax—also passed in 1913. This tax was unconstitutional, so a constitutional amendment was required. The sixteenth amendment was never properly ratified by the required number of states and regardless does not allow for federal taxation of income earned via labor.[15] There is no law that you must pay income taxes. However, via color of law and what basically amounts to contract fraud, by submitting an income tax return Americans subject themselves to the mafia enforcement arm of the Federal Reserve, the Internal Revenue

12 Sir Josiah Stamp, Director of the Bank of England (appointed 1928) and reportedly second wealthiest man in England at that time. http://www.themoneymasters.com/index.htm

13 See Article 1, section 8 of the Constitution.

14 The 2nd plank of the Communist Manifesto is a heavy graduated income tax and the fifth plank is creation of an authoritative central bank. This is not coincidental since "Communism" was just another scam the elite bankers came up with to consolidate money and power.

15 I highly recommend Aaron Russo's documentary *Freedom to Fascism*. He exposes the income tax as a fraud and explains the role of the Federal Reserve.

Service.[16] The income tax was introduced at a seemingly reasonable 1%, but starting in the 1950's has been ratcheted up into the monster that it is today.

The reason that the income tax has increased so drastically is that the interest required to service the national debt has also risen astronomically. The United States is now the most indebted nation in the history of the world. The shift from most prosperous nation in the world to most indebted occurred as a direct result of the Federal Reserve System. Since the Federal Reserve took over, the dollar has lost over 95% of its value. It is also no longer tied to gold, silver, or any other hard asset.[17] The reason that the dollar has not fully collapsed is tied to its use as world reserve currency and the ability of the government to export debt and inflation via the sale of U.S. Treasury Bonds. As of the writing of this book, there are calls from China, Russia, oil producing Middle Eastern countries, and the U.N. for a new world reserve currency, possibly composed of a basket of currencies and partially backed by gold. If and when this happens, the dollar's value will collapse. The only way out from under the massive debt burden for the U.S. Government is to default on the debt (not a viable option), or to pay the debt through monetization, which will result in hyperinflation. Marc Faber, a respected financial analyst, has stated that hyperinflation is inevitable and will likely kick in the next five to ten years (2014-2019).[18] Hyperinflation is of course devastating to an economy because it wipes out savings and makes even the purchase of food an expensive proposition. For example, in the hyperinflation

16 While the income tax is a fraud and some individuals have fought successfully in court to show that they are not required to pay it, I cannot recommend not paying it. Even though it is a criminal organization, it has the power to strip you of all your property and throw you in jail.

17 Purely fiat currencies are not of themselves a bad thing, but they are far more subject to central bank manipulation and to collapse via inflation than gold-backed currencies.

18 See "Marc Faber: 'I am 100% Sure that the U.S. Will Go Into Hyperinflation" on prisonplanet.com http://www.prisonplanet.com/marc-faber-%E2%80%9Ci-am-100-sure-that-the-us-will-go-into-hyperinflation%E2%80%9D.html or "Economist Warns Fed Will Bring About Zimbabwe Style Hyperinflation" by Steve Watson. http://www.prisonplanet.com/economist-warns-fed-will-bring-about-zimbabwe-style-hyperinflation.html

of the Weimar Republic, people spent an average of 92% of household income on food.[19]

So, how exactly was this mess created? Along with the Federal Reserve itself and its manipulation of interest rates, the financial system as a whole is set up for failure. The United States currently has a debt-based monetary system. This means that money is "created" when loans are given out. A common misperception is that banks are in possession of the money that they loan out to people. This is not actually the case. When the bank approves a loan for $100,000, this money is created once the loan is issued. Before the fractional reserve system was manipulated completely out of control, banks were required to have about 10% of what they loaned out on hand as reserves. So, in order to loan out $100,000, they would be required to have in reserve $10,000.[20] This creates an incredibly profitable rate of return on the loan issued. While the borrower is paying 8% interest on their loan, the bank is receiving an 80% return on its $10,000 reserve. While this in itself is an unfair system that benefits banks at the detriment of everyone else (ever wonder why the biggest buildings in your city are always bank offices?), it pales in comparison to what was done to precipitate the financial collapse of 2008.

The corporate media spin on the financial collapse was that it was caused by people defaulting on their sub-prime mortgages. There is a grain of truth to this, but as usual this explanation ignores the bigger picture. The bigger picture is the manipulation of the Federal Reserve and their government cronies. The Federal Reserve has the power to raise or lower interest rates. When rates are kept artificially low, there are many more investors who borrow "cheap money." This always results in mal-investment. For example, the dot com stocks bubble of the 90's.[21] When the dot com bubble burst,

19 Many experts recommend investing in hard assets such as silver and gold and having a large supply of storable food on hand to protect against the ruinous effects of a dollar collapse.

20 Banking reserves can come from deposits or from extremely low interest loans from the Federal Reserve. http://www.answers.com/topic/reserve-requirements

21 There were other factors involved in this bubble as well, such as the removal of requirements (such as profitability) that companies formerly had to meet in order to go public. I recommend "The Great American Bubble Machine" by Matt Taibbi in Rolling Stone 1082-83. http://www.rollingstone.com/politics/story/28816321/the_great_american_bubble_machine#

America should have gone into a serious recession. Instead, Alan Greenspan and the Federal Reserve managed to inflate the housing bubble. This was done via artificially low interest rates, the removal of the Glass-Steagall Act in 1999, government affordable housing programs and requirements, and a media propaganda push. The result of these forces all pushing in the same direction was a lot of new people eligible to buy houses and a lot of investors suddenly interested in real estate speculation. Housing prices soared until 2006 when the Federal Reserve began to tighten the money supply again and people began defaulting on their home loans.

The cause of both the housing boom and the bust, however, also had to do with what banks did with the "assets" created by all the new housing loans. These loans were packaged together and titled "mortgage backed assets." The idea was that instead of selling one risky loan to an investor, you sell a thousand risky loans bundled together and somehow that mitigates the risk. The key to this scam was the complicity of the ratings agencies. They listed what are now called "toxic assets" as AAA, or as good as gold. Big time investors such as the pension fund CalPERS[22] in California were lured in to invest in "safe" real estate investment vehicles which offered much better returns than any other AAA rated asset. The result, of course, was that the market insiders, such as those at Goldman Sachs, pushed the bubble and invested heavily in it on the way up and then shorted it and profited heavily again on the way down. The losers for the most part were anyone with a pension or IRA.

The toxic assets being bundled and sold were not the end of the problem, however. Banks leveraged their holdings many times based on these "assets" and invested heavily in derivative paper and Credit Default Swaps (CDS's). The total amount of derivative paper that is still floating around has been estimated between $596 trillion and $1.5 quadrillion, or $1,500,000,000,000,000.[23] In contrast, the total of real assets in the world is calculated at about $30 trillion and assets including stocks, bonds, and banking deposits at

22 "Calpers to Report Losses of 103% on its Residential Investments" http://globaleconomicanalysis.blogspot.com/2008/12/calpers-to-report-losses-of-103-on-its.html

23 "Is Obama a Wall Street Project" interview of Webster Tarpley on Russia Today. http://www.youtube.com/watch?v=B6OYdqFuTrs&feature=channel_page

$167 trillion.[24] Keep in mind that for every transaction that takes place in the financial world, there are fees and commissions taken out. As Leonard L. Levinson said, "Finance is the art of passing money from one hand to another until it finally disappears."

Manipulating the system and profiting from exchanges of bogus paper was not enough for the Wall Street bankers, however. They also demanded bailouts of government money to keep certain key insider companies going and eliminate competition. A great example of this can be seen by examining the FDIC's collusion with J.P. Morgan to hijack a relatively healthy bank, Washington Mutual, and feed it into a very unhealthy and destructive bank.[25] The TARP program gave money to insider banks and let others be attacked and hijacked by the FDIC. This bill was passed under the threat that martial law would be needed in the streets if it was voted down.[26] The bill also explicitly stated that the decisions made on who received the money and who didn't could not be reviewed or overturned by any other agency in government.[27]

For the elite, the key to keeping this present system going and to eventually failing-forward into an even more powerful international banking system[28] is to make sure that every nation is committed to and reliant on the success of the system. The Anglo-American Empire, the New World Order Empire, is first and foremost a financial empire. Nations that resist the financial system of the New World Order (central bank control, fractional reserve banking, dollar as reserve currency, etc.) are labeled

24 "$596 Trillion! How can the derivatives market be worth more than the world's total financial assets?" by Jacob Leibenluft in Slate Magazine. http://www.slate.com/id/2202263/

25 Check out Frank Lorde's excellent investigative work on this subject. http://www.youtube.com/watch?v=43ZKaW3PZZw , http://wamustory.com/

26 "Democratic Congressman: Representatives Were Threatened With Martial Law in America Over Bailout Bill" by Steve Watson. http://www.infowars.net/articles/october2008/031008Sherman.htm

27 "Bailout is financial equivalent of the Patriot Act" by Andrew Ross Sorkin http://www.infowars.com/bailout-is-financial-equivalent-of-the-patriot-act/?cp=6

28 It appears that the IMF will be the vehicle for the "bank of the world" concept. The Bank of International Settlements (BIS) is also an important player. The heart of all these institutions is the same elite banking families that have been cooperating and inter-marrying for hundreds of years.

"rogue" nations. Do not let the media fool you. When Iraq, Iran, or even Venezuela is targeted it has nothing to do with being an "authoritarian" or "socialist" country. It is because the country's leaders are attempting to stand up to the New World Order banking cartel. The American military industrial and intelligence complex does not work to defend the freedom and security of the American people. It works for Wall Street and for the New World Order banking cartel.[29]

> Banking establishments are more dangerous than standing armies; the principle of spending money to be paid by posterity, under the name of funding, is but swindling futurity on a large scale. – Thomas Jefferson[30]

29 See John Perkins excellent book on this subject based on his own experience in the system, *Confessions of an Economic Hit Man.*

30 http://wiki.monticello.org/mediawiki/index.php/Private_Banks_(Quotation) This is an authenticated version of a longer, more famous Jefferson quote that although partially spurious certainly accurately reflects Jefferson's attitude toward central banks.

## Chapter 5

# The War Machine

"We have been lied to in every military escapade in the last 50 or 60 years, without exception."

– Charles Lewis

"Generals gathered in their masses/ just like witches at black masses.
Evil minds that plot destruction/ sorcerers of death's construction.
In the fields the bodies burning/ as the war machine keeps turning.
Death and hatred to mankind, poisoning their brainwashed minds.
...Satan, laughing, spreads his wings"

– "War Pigs" by Black Sabbath

The mechanics of how we are lied to and tricked into supporting wars will be addressed in later chapters on media propaganda and false flag terrorism. In this chapter, let us briefly examine the war machine itself. The American war machine, also called the military industrial complex,[1] was constructed for the fighting of World War II. War has always been a key tool of the elite. Not only for gaining power and control over people in other lands but also for having a unifying and galvanizing outside threat to keep their own people in-line and following orders.[2] To oversimplify things: war is poor people fighting poor people at the expense of middle class people for the benefit of rich people. Or, as Col. Smedley Butler writes:

1 Please read or watch Dwight D. Eisenhower's farewell address.

2 George Orwell's *1984* makes this point well as does the *Report from Iron Mountain* (whether it is a leaked government report or savvy political satire).

> WAR is a racket. It always has been.
>
> It is possibly the oldest, easily the most profitable, surely the most vicious. It is the only one international in scope. It is the only one in which the profits are reckoned in dollars and the losses in lives.
>
> A racket is best described, I believe, as something that is not what it seems to the majority of the people. Only a small "inside" group knows what it is about. It is conducted for the benefit of the very few, at the expense of the very many. Out of war a few people make huge fortunes.
>
> In the World War [I] a mere handful garnered the profits of the conflict. At least 21,000 new millionaires and billionaires were made in the United States during the World War. That many admitted their huge blood gains in their income tax returns. How many other war millionaires falsified their tax returns no one knows.[3]

The only thing I would argue with Colonel Butler about is that unfortunately war is not the only racket that is international in scope. One key point that Butler makes in a clear and concise manner in his book is that war is the reason we go to war. The elite want war. There does not have to be a good reason for it. Any excuse they can get people to buy into is good enough.

War is the chief means by which nations become indebted to the banks. The U.S., for example, budgeted 54% of its total federal budget to military related expenditures, approximately $1.5 trillion for the 2009 budget. This is more military spending than the next 15 countries combined.[4] Along with cashing in directly on the interest from government loans, banking interests also own large swaths of the military industrial complex. Fortunately for them, they also own large swaths of the government and media as well, so gaining support for war is just not all that difficult to do.[5]

---

3 Smedley Butler exposed the "Business Plot" which was a plan by Prescott Bush and others to form a fascist dictatorship in the U.S. His book and his active denunciation of war helped lead to most American regretting involvement in WWI and in a general non-interventionist sentiment. This was overcome, unfortunately, by a great deal of war propaganda and by the deliberate antagonizing of Japan and the ignoring of warnings about the attack on Pearl Harbor. Butler's excellent little book, *War is a Racket* is available for free online at http://www.lexrex.com/enlightened/articles/warisaracket.htm

4 "Where your income tax money really goes" http://www.warresisters.org/pages/piechart.htm

5 I recommend watching the film *Why We Fight* by Eugene Jarecki, which does a good job outlining what the military industrial complex is and how it functions.

War also gives governments an excuse to crack down on citizens by characterizing dissent as unpatriotic. The Bush administration did this during the Iraq War with the introduction of "free speech zones," which were actually metal cages for protesters. Much of the propaganda was distributed through talking heads on TV and radio. The bastion of journalistic integrity, Bill O'Reilly, stated time and time again that...

> Once the war against Saddam Hussein begins, we expect every American to support our military, and if you can't do that, just shut up. Americans, and indeed our foreign allies who actively work against our military once the war is underway, will be considered enemies of the state by me.[6]

Even occasionally accurate talker Michael Savage suggested using the Sedition Act against war protesters.[7]

The Patriot Act was supposedly passed to protect us from terrorists. However, it has proved to be nothing more than an excuse to disregard civil liberties. For example, it has been used against "toy store proprietors, the homeless, owners of websites, writers, artists, photographers, and common criminals."[8] There are hundreds of examples from America and other countries that reveal the universal tendency of the state is to use crises, including war, to accumulate power and to become more and more oppressive. Is it any surprise, then, to discover that politicians, corporate titans, and powerful bankers work intentionally to create war?

War may well be an inescapable phenomenon in man's sinful, fallen state. However, that does not mean we, as Christians, should support it. Many of us were suckered into supporting wars in Afghanistan and Iraq because our "Christian" president told us we had been attacked by terrorists who hate us for our freedom. And, that we were going to be greeted as liberators. In reality, troops were already massing for the invasion of Afghanistan before September 11th, 2001, and the plans for war in Iraq had

6 Bill O'Reilly as quoted in "Pride and Protest" in the Ithaca Times. http://www.zwire.com/site/news.cfm?newsid=7499705&BRD=1395&PAG=461&dept_id=216620&rfi=6

7 Ibid

8 "Military Commissions Act Does Affect US Citizens" by Alex Jones and Paul Joseph Watson. http://www.prisonplanet.com/articles/october2006/221006doesaffect.htm

already long been percolating as well.[9] As Christ-followers, we are called to be peacemakers[10] and to turn the other cheek. When Christ sent his disciples out, he said "Behold, I send you out as sheep among wolves. Therefore be wise as serpents and harmless as doves."[11] The members of the early church were known for their pacifism and often refused military service.[12] Unfortunately, this changed with the merger of Christianity and political power under Constantine.[13]

Elliott Nesch is an excellent example of the embarrassingly small Christian anti-war movement. Elliot walked from Denver to Washington D.C. in order to protest "Christians who support the war."[14] We cannot possibly lend our support for wars that are simply for power and profit. It is time for Christians to become wise to the "foxes" in power, just as Jesus was wise to the tricks of Herod. By falling for the lies of George W. Bush, Donald Rumsfeld, Dick Cheney, Barack Obama, and their puppet masters, we have sent the message to the rest of the world that America, the "Christian Nation," supports war, conquest, and oppression of others. This message must be countered by spreading messages of truth.[15] War is a product of the kingdoms of this world. Those of us who seek to spread the Kingdom of God cannot simultaneously support wars of aggression and expect our message to be well-received.

9 "Actor Charlie Sheen Questions Official 9/11 Story" by Alex Jones and Paul Joseph Watson. http://www.prisonplanet.com/articles/march2006/200306charliesheen.htm

10 Matthew 5:9

11 Matthew 10:16

12 "A Practical Christian Pacifism" by David A. Hoekema. http://www.religion-online.org/showarticle.asp?title=115

13 Ibid

14 *The 9/11 Chronicles: Part One, Truth Rising* produced by Alex Jones. Tells the story of the 9/11 truth movement and traces activities of those involved. http://www.youtube.com/watch?v=t-yscpNIxjI&feature=channel Also, check out the YouTube video "Elliott Nesch: Pro War Christians Should Repent!" http://www.youtube.com/watch?v=qYAdsAiwpBc

15 Check out Adam Kokesh and the organization Iraq Veterans Against the War. www.ivaw.com

# Chapter 6
# Pseudo-Science

Foreign policy is not the only area where the controllers of government and its institutions have been lying to us. Modern western society has seen the "orthodoxy" of the Roman Catholic Church replaced with the "secular" god of science. One of the tenets of this book is that good science and a serious, straightforward reading of the Bible do not contradict each other. It is unfortunate that many Christians (myself included), have at one time or another felt afraid that science would weaken our faith if we examined its findings closely. True science, however, based on empirical data, experimentation, understanding the laws of nature, etc, has done nothing to undermine the Bible. In many cases the opposite is true. Science often reinforces Biblical truths.

For example, the Big Bang theory established very convincingly the idea that the universe had a beginning. This was a surprise to most scientists who had long based their understanding of the universe on the idea that the material universe was eternal (while the Greeks are often credited with this concept, it was popular in the earliest recorded civilizations). Christians were not surprised by this scientific breakthrough, of course, because Genesis clearly states that the universe had a beginning and that God spoke it into existence.

String theory, the cutting edge of modern physics, is based on the idea that tiny vibrating strings are the foundational elements of the universe.[1] This sounds a bit like a type of "sound" waves, does it not? Physicists will soon be claiming that the universe

1 See *The Elegant Universe* by Brian Greene.

"spoke itself" into existence if things continue on their current trajectory. In this chapter what I want to examine is not good science. But, instead, pseudo-science that is funded, promoted, and applied for political, social, and spiritual ends.

The two examples of pernicious and satanically driven pseudo-science that we will look at are the theory of macro-evolution and the theory of anthropomorphic global warming (AGW). Christians have long battled the teachings of evolution for obvious reasons. But, many professing Christians have embraced the theory of anthropomorphic global warming.

When we examine these two theories, we can see that they have several things in common. They both assume that man is the ultimate actor in the universe and eschew the possibility that God or any other spiritual being[2] impacts the direction of life on earth. Both are virulently anti-human and view mankind as an accidental scourge upon the earth. Both hold that the deaths of massive numbers of people would have substantial benefits as far as improving life on earth. Both are accepted as veritas by the corporate media and therefore anyone who questions them is ridiculed, attacked, and dismissed as completely irrational and backwards. And, perhaps most intriguing of all, both are based on very shoddy and unscientific reasoning.

It was actually the similarity of media propaganda that first helped me make the connection between anthropomorphic global warming and macro-evolution. I had been back and forth on the whole evolution debate without ever really studying the issue. Growing up, I was homeschooled and went to a small Christian school where creation science was taught. My senior year of high school (I was then in public school), I took an Advanced Biology course where evolution was assumed, but never really explained. At Grand Canyon University I took several classes from Dr. David Reiter who was a big proponent of Intelligent Design Theory. But, I was also exposed to a professor who was a professing Christian, but a staunch advocate of evolution. The end result, I must admit, was that at some points in my life I was media-brainwashed enough to believe the lie that evolution was scientifically-proven and that I needed to adapt my Christian beliefs and understand-

2 Their official presentation is materialistic and scientific, but their most strident proponents are very spiritually driven as we will look at later.

ing of the Bible to try and fit evolution. I was told over and over again through the media that there were mountains of evidence for evolution. And, that anyone who didn't believe it was just an unenlightened, close-minded crackpot.

Similarly, I hadn't really looked into the claims of global warming. Yet, I assumed it was true because of the constant repetition of it in the corporate media, in academia, and in the materials I used as a public school teacher. The shocking truth is that both macro-evolution and anthropomorphic global warming have very little scientific support.[3] Adherence to these theories is obtained through the pressure of very powerful financial interests that can be traced back to the same banking families that have been ruling from behind the scenes for hundreds of years. The "scientific consensus" on both of these issues is nothing but a manufactured myth.

In a perfect world, scientists would have all the funding they wanted to study any phenomenon they wanted with no other agenda than to seek the truth about the way the material world functions. This, however, is not the way science works in our world. Funding comes either directly from governments in the form of grants, indirectly from government through universities, from corporations, or from the foundations. All of these groups are interconnected, and all of them answer to the same financial elite. In recent years (once AGW gained favor among the elite for reasons to be discussed later), scientists have found that if they want to get research funding then it is highly advisable that they work global warming into their research proposals.[4] Because of this, there are numerous mentions of global warming in scientific literature even though most of the scientists aren't really studying global warming directly.

The companies that produce textbooks must remain absolutely aware of what is politically correct and to avoid like the plague anything that would make public educational institutions

3 Check out "What is the Evidence for Evolution?" on Berkeley's website and see if you are impressed. I certainly wasn't. http://evolution.berkeley.edu/evolibrary/search/topicbrowse2.php?topic_id=46 I also looked for websites purporting scientific evidence for anthropomorphic global warming but there is extremely little in the way of real science anywhere to support this idea.

4 The Great Global Warming Swindle (an excellent documentary that exposes the fraudulent claims that AGW theorists commonly make). http://video.google.com/videoplay?docid=288952680655100870

hesitant to purchase their materials. It is clearly politically incorrect to challenge AGW, and highly profitable to treat AGW as fact and as a grave danger to humanity. Consequently, virtually every children's textbook in America—or anywhere else the United Nations controls education—is filled with global warming fear-mongering.

The corporate media must also subscribe to the "politically correct" version of reality and promulgate it constantly. Most large news agencies even have reporters or whole divisions dedicated to environmental issues. Because the elite want to keep the focus off of real environmental problems that they are causing, they keep the focus on the imaginary evils of AGW. A reporter who is trying to sell their story will of course seek out the most extreme proponents of the theory, such as Al Gore or James Hansen, in order to justify an attention-grabbing story. The educational establishment and corporate media create the "reality" of AGW through repetition and scare-mongering rather than actual science.

Al Gore fired Dr. Will Happer, an AGW skeptic, from his job at the U.S. Department of Energy. Gore then told him, "Science must not intrude on public policy."[5] As Gore admits, AGW is not about careful and exact scientific research, it is about creating support for public policy. This public policy was created by several groups within the secret (and much more powerful) government. This shadow government consists of those who control the Bilderberg Group, the Club of Rome, the Trilateral Commission, and the Council on Foreign Relations.

> In 1990, writes veteran reporter Jim Tucker, the Bilderbergers adopted climate change as the preferred model to impose global government and reintroduce serfdom. "Like the Trilateral Commission, the Bilderberg Group discovered the issue of environmental deterioration. Bilderbergers embraced a report from the Trilateral Commission that year on the environment, because the potential profit in cleaning up the mess would be immense."
>
> The following year, the Club of Rome think tank published *The First Global Revolution*, a book suggesting a draconian neo-Mal-

5 "Princeton Physicist Calls Global Warming Science 'Mistaken'" by Michael Asher of Daily Tech. http://www.prisonplanet.com/princeton-physicist-calls-global-warming-science-mistaken.html

> thusianism approach will solve the world's "problems", in fact a problem the global elite has with humanity.
>
> "In searching for a new enemy to unite us, we came up with the idea that pollution, the threat of global warming, water shortages, famine and the like would fit the bill," the book states. "All these dangers are caused by human intervention," and thus the "real enemy, then, is humanity itself."
>
> Richard Haass, the current president of the Council on Foreign Relations, expanded on this topic in his article, "State sovereignty must be altered in a globalized era." According to Haass, a system of world government must be created and sovereignty eliminated in order to fight global warming and terrorism, both invented as the Club of Rome suggested.
>
> "Some governments are prepared to give up elements of sovereignty to address the threat of global climate change," writes Haass. "The goal should be to redefine sovereignty for the era of globalization, to find a balance between a world of fully sovereign states and an international system of either world government or anarchy."[6]

As we can see from Steve Watson's article, the agenda behind AGW is creating a "common enemy" for mankind as a means of creating the impetus and excuse for global governance. The anti-human propaganda element of AGW is also revealing; perhaps Satan's hatred of mankind rubs off on his minions. Legislation to "combat climate change" is really part of a plan to use carbon taxes to fund a world bank and set up the necessary framework for world government.

AGW shares its anti-human agenda with evolution. After all, if we are nothing but a cosmic coincidence and there is no inherent value to human life, then everything is permissible. Man is his own judge and can construct a system of morality to suit him. Evolution presents Satan's oldest lie in a quasi-scientific manner; it tells us that we can keep evolving and eventually become gods. Satan has long presented this lie in many false religions, such as Hinduism. This is the dream of the New World Order elite. They believe that they can shape mankind's evolution and that they can attain complete control and eventually

6 "Obama Intimately Tied To Carbon Trading Scam" by Steve Watson http://blog.oldthinkernews.com/?p=65

immortality. In the next chapter, we will look at how evolution laid the philosophical groundwork for the system of thought that has been the obsessive dream of the elite for the last 150 years, eugenics.

## Chapter 7

# The Theory of Eugenics

> The wisest thing in the world is to cry out before you are hurt. It is no good to cry out after you are hurt; especially after you are mortally hurt. People talk about the impatience of the populace; but sound historians know that most tyrannies have been possible because men moved too late. It is often essential to resist a tyranny before it exists. It is no answer to say, with a distant optimism, that the scheme is only in the air. A blow from a hatchet can only be parried while it is in the air.
>
> –G.K. Chesterton[1]

Unfortunately for humanity, Chesterton's cries about eugenics and the path it would lead the state down went largely unheeded. As a result, the hatchet blows to mankind have included the Holocaust and carnage of WWII, forced sterilization of thousands upon thousands of women in countries ranging from Canada to China, from Africa to the United States, over 50 million abortions in the U.S. alone, and a general degeneration of the perceived value of human life.

Eugenics is the natural offspring of Darwinism.[2] While eugenic ideology can be traced back to Plato's *Republic*, it was Dar-

1 *Eugenics and Other Evils* by G.K. Chesterton: First published in 1922, this book is an excellent rebuttal to the foundational beliefs and assumptions of eugenics. Chesterton's foresight has been (unfortunately) proven right in spades.

2 Darwinism itself is of course not the origin of evolutionary theory, but I am focusing on this particular incarnation of an age-old lie. Also, eugenics is not the only harmful child of evolution. The others include social Darwinism, monopolistic capitalism (as opposed to free market), materialism, consumerism, etc.

win's cousin, Francis Galton, who in 1865 began propagating the ideas that would become known as eugenics. Both eugenics and evolution are pseudo-scientific attempts to justify what has long been the behavior of political elites: inbreeding among themselves and the oppression of other people. The basic theory of eugenics is that man can help natural selection along by encouraging the strongest and smartest specimens of the human species to breed while halting the reproduction of "inferior" humans. In this manner, it was theorized, humanity would progress ever more rapidly toward a more advanced and even "perfected" state. Isn't it amazing how the original lie of Satan (that we can become gods through advanced knowledge and our own volition) still permeates all of his programs today?

Eugenics was popular with robber barons such as Rockefeller, Morgan, Ford, and the rest of the elite for the same reasons Darwinian evolution was popular. It provided pseudo-scientific reasons for inbreeding among the elites, for oppression and exploitation of the poor, and for placing themselves in the place of the one true God as masters of humanity. God, thanks to Darwinism, had become unnecessary and His existence could even be denied. The most powerful of the elites, as has been the case throughout history, were not atheists but were instead Luciferians, having joined Lucifer in his rebellion for the promise of control of the kingdoms of this world and for the false hope of becoming gods.[3] While the elites certainly cannot be described as atheists, they used and continue to use the philosophies of materialism and evolution to separate people from belief in God.

The rank and file eugenicist, as Chesterton points out, genuinely thinks that eugenics will improve society. But, "evil always wins through the strength of its splendid dupes."[4] As I attempt to point out throughout this book, it is the Satan-influenced elites who set the agenda and their hierarchical structures of state, foundation, and secret society power that carry it out. Of the well intentioned but naïve and deceived autocrats, Chesterton

3 I will back up this assertion of elites being involved in worshipping Satan with more evidence later in the book, but if you doubt this please research world leaders and their occult activities.

4 *Eugenics and Other Evils* by G.K. Chesterton, p. 14

says, "Of these it is enough to say that they do not understand the nature of a law anymore than the nature of a dog. If you let loose a law, it will do as a dog does. It will obey its own nature, not yours."[5]

Chesterton's observation accurately presents the danger of passing any law that allows the state to impede personal liberty, but was especially prescient in regards to eugenics legislation. The Mental Deficiency Act of 1913, the U.S. Immigration Restriction Act of 1924, and forced sterilization laws in a majority of states were exactly the types of laws that Chesterton feared letting loose.[6] The sterilization laws were administered by eugenics courts, the forerunners of the modern extra-judicial family courts.

The true agenda behind this legislation can be seen in the words of Major Leonard Darwin's lecture to the Cambridge University Eugenics Society in 1912. "It is quite certain that no existing democratic government would go as far as we Eugenists think right in the direction of limiting the liberty of the subject for the sake of the racial qualities of future generations."[7] Darwin also asserts the idea that the "mentally abnormal" be rooted out through the educational and prison systems.[8] It is impossible to miss the relevancy of Darwin's statement when we consider the fact that the U.S. has the largest prisoner population in the world. And, when we examine the ever-increasing number of "syndromes" and "disorders" that are causing the number of special education students to continue to rise, it is clear that the Eugenicists are in charge. As we can see today and by looking at the wreckage of the past century, the aims of eugenics are incompatible with personal liberty. Liberty, free will, and human equality[9] are ideas that go hand in hand, and they are all anathema to the eugenics state.[10]

---

5 Ibid, 22

6 Please see www.eugenicsarchive.org for a comprehensive list of eugenics legislation in America

7 *Eugenics and Other Evils* 145

8 Ibid 144

9 Human equality is a relatively rare idea in history that can be credited to Judeo-Christian thought.

10 By "eugenics state" I am referring not only to the official government, but to the entire apparatus of power (secret societies, tax-free foundations, etc.)

Materialistic determinism is at the heart of the ideology of the eugenics state; along with its contradictory but corresponding assertions that evolution can be quickened and guided by the state. Chesterton makes this assertion about the prevailing materialistic view of world events.

> The mark of the atheistic style is that it instinctively chooses the word which suggests that things are dead things; that things have no souls. Thus they will not speak of waging war, which means willing it; they speak of the "outbreak of war," as if all the guns blew up without the men touching them.[11]

This denial of human or divine causality has become endemic in academic portrayals of history, anthropology, science, and even economics (the "naturally occurring" business cycle). When human causes are admitted, they are framed as brief accidents (e.g. Hitler's reign of terror), rather than as the result of much planning and a coherent ideology. Many people even use the expression "never ascribe to conspiracy what can be attributed to accident or incompetence" to "debunk" the intentional view of history. Franklin D. Roosevelt recognized the idiocy of the "coincidence" view of history and politics. He said, "In politics, nothing happens by accident. If it happens, you can bet it was planned that way."[12] While many consequences may be unintended, the initiating events are not caused by accidents or coincidences.

Hitler, who was a fawning admirer of American eugenicists such as Margaret Sanger and Madison Grant,[13] used eugenics to justify his racist ideologies and set about creating his infamous "master race." The backlash to Hitler's hideous but eugenically logical applications of this theory drove the eugenicists to hide their agenda behind more carefully camouflaged propaganda, programs, and titles. Eugenics did not end with Hitler's death, as we can see by the following statements.

11 *Eugenics and Other Evils* 40

12 http://www.brainyquote.com/quotes/quotes/f/franklind164126.html

13 Hitler called Grant's book *The Passing of the Great Race* his "bible." See "The Roaring 20's and the Roots of American Fascism: American Eugenics" http://www.spiritone.com/~gdy52150/1920sp6.html

> The [Eugenics] Society should pursue eugenic ends by less obvious means, that is by a policy of crypto-eugenics, which was apparently proving successful in the US Eugenics Society.[14]
>
> I think we have failed to take into account a trait which is almost universal and is very deep in human nature. People simply are not willing to accept the idea that the genetic base on which their character was formed is inferior and should not be repeated in the next generation. We have asked whole groups of people to accept this idea and we have asked individuals to accept it. They have constantly refused and we have all but killed the eugenic movement . . . they won't accept the idea that they are in general second rate. We must rely on other motivation. [I]t is surely possible to build a system of voluntary unconscious selection. But the reasons advanced must be generally acceptable reasons. Let us stop telling anyone that they have a genetically inferior genetic quality, for they will never agree. Let us base our proposals on the desirability of having children born in homes where they will get affectionate and responsible care, and perhaps our proposals will be accepted. It seems to me that if it is to progress as it should, eugenics must follow new policies and state its case anew, and that from this rebirth we may, even in our own lifetime, see it moving at last towards the high goals which Galton set for it.[15]
>
> "Eugenic goals are most likely to be attained under a name other than eugenics."[16]

It is more difficult to combat eugenics now because it hides behind a plethora of different guises. The underlying philosophical assumptions remain, however, and these we can and must refute at every opportunity.

The eugenics state springs from the basic assumption that the health of the individual is the concern and responsibility of the state. While this may sound innocuous, or even benevolent, Chesterton points out that "if a man's personal health is a public concern, [then] his most private acts are more public that his

---

14 The Activities of the Eugenics Society by Faith Schenk and A.S. Parker, Eugenics Review (1968), vol. 60, no. 3 (these quotes are taken from www.whatistheendgame.com, a bibliography for Alex Jones' excellent film *Endgame: Blueprint for Global Enslavement*

15 "Galton and Mid Century Eugenics" by Frederick Osborn, *Eugenics Review* (1956), vol, 48, no. 1

16 *Future of Human Heredity* (1968) by Frederick Osborn, p. 104

most public acts."[17] When the state is given the power to "protect" the individual from himself, the door is opened for greater and greater tyranny.

> If the men who had denied one liberty had taken the opportunity to affirm other liberties, there might be some defense for them. But it never crosses their minds. Hence the excuse for the last oppression will always serve as well for the next oppression; and to that tyranny there can be no end.[18]

The power to regulate is the power to control. Political power over individuals is predictably dangerous will predictably fall into evil hands. Therefore, we must work to see that the power of the state is as limited as possible regarding personal health and freedom.

17 *Eugenics and Other Evils* 103
18 Ibid 102

## Chapter 8

# The Eugenics Wars: Oppression of the Nanny State

One current nickname for what is really the eugenics state is the "nanny state." Drug laws, alcohol prohibition, smoking laws, trans-fats laws, and many other laws and color of law regulations are gateways through which the bureaucrats of the eugenics state seek greater control. They, and the greater tyrannies that follow, are all based on the foundational assumption that the state has the right to regulate what you do to your own body.

Abortion, ironically, is the one area where eugenics supporters will wax poetic about the rights of a woman to decide what happens to her own body. Where is this argument when it comes to drugs, or, for that matter, drinking raw milk? Abortion, of course, should be illegal because it is not merely the woman's body but her baby's life that is at stake. The true character of the eugenics state and its cheerleaders are revealed in abortion and sterilization.

After WWI, there were several eugenics organizations that were operating openly in the United States. One of the most powerful and most controversial of these groups was the American Birth Control League. This organization counted Margaret Sanger among its leadership.[1] The American Birth Control League focused on state laws that required forced sterilization of the supposed "unfit." These laws were upheld by the Supreme Court in Buck vs. Bell (1927). The Court's opinion, written by Oliver Wendell Holmes, infamously stated that "three generations

1 "The History of Planned Parenthood" by Mike Perry is an excellent article that also contains important references to related material. http://www.ewtn.com/library/PROLIFE/PPHISTRY.TXT

of imbeciles are enough." The American Birth Control League changed its name to Planned Parenthood as a public relations ploy but not as a sign of shifting policy. Mike Perry describes Planned Parenthood's evolving strategy for eliminating as much of the Black, and later, Hispanic population as possible.

> Reaching these people with birth control required new tactics. As the 1940 symposium title hints, "race building" in a democracy has to be subtle. Coercion cannot be overt. Deception must take the place of force. The victims must never know they are a target. A number of tactics were used to deceive the victims.[2]

These new tactics included the recruitment and payment of black leaders and ministers to be the face of Planned Parenthood in the black communities. Margaret Sanger explained the reason for this approach in a letter to Clarence Gamble. "We do not want the word to go out that we want to exterminate the Negro population and the minister is the man who can straighten out the idea if it ever occurs to any of their more rebellious members."[3] Planned Parenthood has since the 60's become very successfully enmeshed in the political and social "mainstream." It was these political alliances that allowed the legalization of abortion and the framing of abortion as a woman's rights issue. While enjoying fawning coverage in the corporate media, alternative and Christian media sources have published stories that decry such things as Planned Parenthood's open acceptance of racist donations.[4] While accepting donations specifically for the killing of black babies is outrageous, it fits perfectly with Planned Parenthood's eugenics agenda.

> No other ethnic group in the United States has been decimated more by abortion than the Afro-American community. The war being waged upon innocent captives in the womb is led by Planned Parenthood.[5]

The claim of Rev. Childress is borne out by the fact that in 2005, black women were 4.8 times as likely to have an abortion as

---

2 Ibid

3 Ibid

4 "Report: Planned Parenthood Accepts Racist Donations" by Katherine Pipp of Baptist Press http://www.bpnews.net/BPnews.asp?ID=27572

5 "Margaret Sanger Would Have Loved Barack Obama" by Rev. Clenard H. Childress Jr. on www.blackgenocide.org (an excellent anti-eugenics site) http://www.blackgenocide.org/obama.html

white women.[6] This is certainly not an accident on the part of the eugenics state.

Let us examine how the eugenics state attacks an individual woman, whom we'll call Jane, and her potential family. Jane lives in a low-income area, is not married, and is pregnant. While Jane is certainly responsible for her own decisions that put her in this predicament, the eugenics state has already been at work for some time in her life. She quite likely grew up in a single-parent household. Media messages promoting sexual promiscuity have bombarded her from early childhood until the present. Her lack of a father has left her more susceptible to the feeling (reinforced in the media) that she "needs" a man around who is attracted to her. Now she is faced with the decision of whether or not to abort her baby. The eugenics state makes abortion readily available. There is, of course, a Planned Parenthood location in her neighborhood. Information on adoption and quality pre-natal care are much harder to come by, even though there are thousands of childless couples who would gladly adopt her baby. Also notably absent in the propaganda from Planned Parenthood is the information about the increased risk of cancer and future infertility associated with abortion. Thankfully, even though the eugenics state agents at Planned Parenthood tell her that her baby is nothing more than a blob of tissue, Jane decides to have her baby and raise him as best she can.

Jane's baby is born. He has blood taken from him which unbeknownst to Jane will be sent to the local health department and will likely find its way into a U.N. database as part of the eugenicists' efforts to map the human genome.[7] He is injected with Hepatitis B vaccine 12 hours after birth,[8] even though Jane has tested negative for Hepatitis B and there is no danger of her baby contracting it. If this vaccine does not kill him,[9] he will still be at a greater risk of developing auto-immune diseases, learn-

6 "Report: Planned Parenthood Accepts Racist Donations" by Katherine Pipp of Baptist Press http://www.bpnews.net/BPnews.asp?ID=27572

7 This project is run out of Cold Spring Harbor, which has long been a bastion of eugenics. http://www.cshl.edu/public/genome.html

8 http://www.vaccineinformation.org/hepb/qandavax.asp (a pro-vaccine propaganda site that admits all children are given the Hepatitis B vaccine even when the risk of contracting Hepatitis is virtually 0%.

9 Read the story of Lyla Rose Belkin. http://thinktwice.com/hepb.htm

ing disabilities, attention deficit disorders, diabetes, asthma, and seizure disorders.[10] Jane will be encouraged by nurses—who get legal kickbacks from infant formula companies—to put her baby on melamine laced formula rather than breastfeeding.[11]

As Jane's son grows up, she will be bombarded with attempts by the eugenics state to fill him with more vaccines. If she avoids having the eugenics state kidnap him directly for any number of minor issues, she will still likely be suckered into placing him into public educational systems beginning with pre-school programs like Head Start. Her child will then be conditioned to conform to his "peer group," and his individuality will be stamped out of him for the most part. He will be exposed to the same media and government education propaganda that Jane was subjected to growing up and unfortunately will likely play his part in repeating the cycle. Jane and her son's only hope, as it is for all of us, is that Jesus Christ gets a hold of her life and breaks through all the conditioning of the satanic eugenics state.

All of the state abuse of Jane and of the rest of us is made possible because of the assumption that the health and well-being of the individual is the responsibility of the state. It comes from the belief that children are ultimately the property of the state rather than the responsibility of their parents.[12] It is time for us to recognize that the state does not love us. The state is not our friend. The state is not our mother. The state is under the manipulation of Satan and the kingdoms of this world. We would be wise to endeavor to keep the powers of the state securely locked in a constitutional cage; guarded by informed and educated citizens who love liberty.

---

10 "School Nurses Speak Out On Hepatitis B Vaccine" by Patti White, R.N. http://www.vaccinationnews.com/DailyNews/June2001/SchoolNursesSpeakOut.htm

11 "90% of U.S. Infant Formula May Be Contaminated With Melamine" by Mike Adams http://www.naturalnews.com/024947.html The article goes on to point out that while previously the FDA stated there was no safe level of melamine, after the revelation that 90% of formula was contaminated the FDA pulled the number one part per million the FDA as a "safe" exposure level and began prohibiting testing below this level. Formula has also been associated with smaller brain size and IQ reduction in many studies.

12 "Homeschooling Banned In California As State Turns Parents Into Criminals for Teaching Their Own Children" by David Gutierrez, available on www.prisonplanet.com (Fortunately, this ruling was later overturned. However, it reveals the attitude of the state and of the bureaucrats that operate it).

Jack McLamb and others have often said, "when tyranny comes to your door, it will be wearing a uniform." I agree wholeheartedly with this statement and I would add that when tyranny comes to your door, it will probably justify its actions as for the good of your children or for your health. One of the trademarks of the eugenics state is what Chesterton calls the "kidnapping of children upon the most fantastic excuses of sham psychology."[13] In the U.S., the state-sponsored and sanctioned kidnapping is carried out by the Orwellian Child Protective Services.

Child Protective Services (CPS) was the requisite enforcement arm that grew out of the eugenics courts. CPS has been rapidly growing as government agencies are wont to do, and is kidnapping children for an ever expanding number of reasons. Your child was bitten by the neighbor's dog? Say goodbye to all your kids, even if you can prove the CPS worker deliberately lied about your case.[14] Your eight year old child has a small bruise on her leg from bumping into a table? CPS will strip search her; find nothing, and still try to take your kids.[15] Of course, these cases are rarely publicized in the corporate media. When the issue is covered, it is nearly always parents who are the enemy either because they are abusive or are drug addicts. No one would argue that children should have a safe and stable home in which to grow up. But, is this provided by the eugenics state?

> Child protective agencies nationwide are forcibly removing more children from their homes even when the agencies' own investigations establish that the children have not been abused or neglected, according to reports submitted by state agencies to the National Center on Child Abuse and Neglect (NCCAN) during 1998. Once in foster care, state agencies further reported, children were much more likely to be maltreated than they are in their own homes.
>
> Family advocates blame financial incentives offered through new federal legislation for the frightening trend that places increas-

13 *Eugenics and Other Evils*, p. 111

14 Sadly, this is the real life case of Greg Pound and his family. www.rescuemykids.com

15 "Texas Authorities Deny Strip-Search of Eight Year Old Girl" by Patrick George of the American Statesman. http://www.infowars.com/texas-authorites-deny-strip-search-of-8-year-old/

> ing numbers of families at risk of losing their children and a national watchdog organization has pledged to use NCCAN's statistics to alert parents.
>
> Children are eleven times more likely to be sexually abused in state care than they are in their own homes, according to NCCAN. While 59 out of 100,000 children in the general population are alleged to be physically abused, 160 — more than twice as much — were physically abused in the foster care population. Neglect? The 32 states submitting data in this category reported that 490 per hundred thousand children were neglected in their homes and 760 per hundred thousand were neglected in state care. Tragically, 6.4 children per 100,000 were killed in foster care in 1998 compared to a rate of 1.5 per hundred thousand in the general population.[16]

As the above article points out, children are much more likely to be abused while in state care than the rate for the general population. In addition, up to half of children who are state care are there because of admittedly unsubstantiated abuse.[17] Specific examples of state sponsored abuse are plentiful. One such example is the behavior of the Texas Youth Commission. Government officials sexually and physically abused young inmates with relative impunity until the story finally broke in the press.[18]

One of the most frequent excuses used by the eugenics state to kidnap children is drug use by the children's parents. Ironically, the eugenics state is much more likely to place children on legal but very dangerous drugs like Prozac or Ritalin. For example, in Texas, two out of three foster children are on psychotropic drugs, with some children on as many as 17 drugs at once.[19] When trying to explain why so many children are placed on psychotropic drugs while in government custody, Dr. Joseph Burkett said, "A

16 "Dorothy's Never Coming Home: New Law Puts Families in Crisis" from CPS Watch http://familyrightsassociation.com/bin/white_papers-articles/dorothy_never_coming_home/

17 Ibid

18 See the website of the Dallas Morning News in the Investigative Reports section. "Scandal At TYC" http://www.dallasnews.com/investigativereports/tyc/

19 "Two Out of Three Foster Children in Texas on Psychotropic Medication" from a TV news report by WOAI http://www.infowars.com/articles/brave_new_world/fosterkids_drugs.htm

lot of these kids come from bad gene pools."[20] It is not hard to see the eugenics and nanny state mindset of this doctor and others who aid this system. The reason that foster parents often push to have children in their care placed on these drugs is that government offers extra financial assistance for the care of children with mental health designations.

The love of money is the driving force that Satan uses to get many people who are not conscious of the New World Order system to serve it. This is certainly the case in the eugenics state when it comes to Child Protective Services. States are given funding based on meeting ever increasing targets of child seizures. Therefore, agencies generally compensate the CPS caseworkers according to how many kidnappings they are able to carry out. In addition, private adoption agencies also offer large bounties to state agencies in exchange for prized children (in some cases up to $400,000 for a blond haired, blue eyed child). While many people join CPS with the best of intentions, those folks do not last very long when they see the gut-wrenching corruption of the system. This explains the amazingly high turnover rate for CPS caseworkers. Along with those motivated by avarice, the other group that stays in the system is pedophiles. There is no better place to gain access to vulnerable children than by working in Child Protective Services. While most people cannot imagine having to take someone's children away from them on a daily basis, the greed-driven and pedophilia-driven CPS case workers revel in their service to the satanic eugenics state.[21]

The eugenics state does not stop with kidnapping children. Satan and the lust for political power drive its bureaucrats and henchman to seek many ways of enrolling people in the system. The poor are the main target, with millions of people getting sucked into the juvenile correction system and the rest of the prison industrial complex.

---

20 "Groups Criticize Remark about 'Bad Gene Pools'" by Polly Ross Hughes of the *Houston Chronicle* http://www.amren.com/mtnews/archives/2004/10/groups_criticiz.php

21 The source for the above paragraph is many interviews of people including state senators, former CPS employees, victimized parents, and expert lawyers that Alex Jones has conducted on *The Alex Jones Show*.

If you want to see the ultimate goal of the eugenics state, visit a prison. Individuality is not permitted. Behavior is tightly restricted and regimented. All areas of life—from eating, to sleeping, to showering, are carried out in a controlled and collective environment designed to squash individual freedom. Work is required at slave wages that benefits private corporations who then offer bribes to politicians to keep the system going. Even teenagers are sent to work camps for minor or non-existent offenses. The judges that send them there receive kickbacks from the private contractors who run the camps and receive funding from government.[22] The prison industrial complex is even more exploitative, with the most extreme example being the formerly classified Civilian Inmate Labor Program. Prisoners are taken to secret military-run camps in exchange for signing non-disclosure forms and shortened sentences.[23] This program is an experiment for a larger labor and internment camp program that is planned as American society falls apart.[24]

When we look carefully at "child protection" and "correctional" systems in America, it is hard to argue with Chesterton when he says "crime is not a disease. It is criminology that is a disease."[25] Even if we manage to avoid the overt systems of the eugenics state, however, we are not immune from its attacks.

22 "Pa. Judges Accused of Jailing Kids for Cash" in the Associated Press. http://www.infowars.com/pa-judges-accused-of-jailing-kids-for-cash/

23 "Civilian Inmate Labor Program http://www.army.mil/usapa/epubs/pdf/r210_35.pdf

24 *Camp FEMA* is a documentary film from producer Gary Franchi and director William Lewis on this topic. FEMA Camps are certainly a reality, although there is much disinformation that the corporate media (such as Glenn Beck) likes to point at in attempts to debunk real information discussed by Alex Jones and others.

25 *Eugenics and Other Evils* p. 111

# Chapter 9

# The Eugenics Wars: We Are All Enemy Combatants

"A total population of 250-300 million people, a 95% decline from present levels, would be ideal."

—Ted Turner[1]

"In the event I am reincarnated, I would like to return as a deadly virus, in order to contribute something to solve overpopulation."

—Prince Philip[2]

Eugenics is at the heart of the philosophical and religious beliefs of the satanic world elite. While usually hiding behind the guise of environmentalism and sustainability, crypto-eugenics is a dominant force behind world political and social policy. These programs at first seem unrelated and are treated, even by some of the people fighting them, as unfortunate accidents. If eugenics and the population reduction agenda are not taken into account, it is impossible for us to make sense of what is going around us. We see skyrocketing rates of cancer, infertility, and a general dumbing down of the population as a whole. In this chapter, we will examine some of the eugenics programs that at-

1 This statement was originally published in *Audubon Magazine*, but is reprinted in "Ted Turner: World Needs a 'Voluntary' One-Child Policy for the Next Hundred Years" by Aaron Dykes. http://www.infowars.com/ted-turner-confronted-by-philly-911-truth/

2 This quote is taken from his biography *If I Were an Animal*, and is quoted here from the article "The Population Reduction Agenda for Dummies" by Paul Joseph Watson. http://www.prisonplanet.com/the-population-reduction-agenda-for-dummies.html

tack the water we drink, the food we eat, the air we breathe, and the vaccines we inject.

John Holdren, who was named President Obama's science czar in 2009, advocated "adding a sterilant to drinking water" in his 1977 government policy textbook *Ecoscience*.[3] The evidence for this recommendation having been followed is clear.

> Global sperm counts have dropped by a third since 1989 and by half in the past 50 years. The rate of decline is only accelerating as more and more couples find it harder to have children. In studies of white European men, the rate of decline is as much as 50 per cent in the last 30 years.[4]

One of many culprits for this drop in sperm counts as well as the increase in female infertility may be the addition of Antiandrogens to the water supply.[5] Antiandrogens are given to sex offenders and men who wish to become women because they inhibit the masculine effects of testosterone. To my knowledge, however, I do not think we ever voted to have them added to our water supplies.

The eugenicists attack our drinking water not only by putting sterilization agents directly into the water supply, but also into the containers from which we drink. It strains credulity to believe it coincidental that out of the hundreds of types of plastics developed by the 1950's, the one that was chosen for nearly universal adoption in plastic bottles leeches an estrogen-mimicking hormone called Biphenyl A. Biphenyl A attacks the sperm count in men and causes an increase in sperm abnormality and testicular cancer. In women, it contributes to early onset puberty, breast cancer, and other problems.[6] The eugenicists' main targets for destruction are reproduction and intelligence. So, it is no surprise that other water additives are used to attack our cognitive capacity.

---

3 "Obama Science Czar's Plan to Sterilize Population Through Water Supply Already Happening" by Paul Joseph Watson. This is an excellent article that contains many direct quotes from Holdren's book as well as links that clearly show this policy is being followed today. http://www.prisonplanet.com/obama-science-czars-plan-to-sterilize-population-through-water-supply-already-happening.html

4 Ibid

5 Ibid

6 *The Disappearing Male*, an excellent documentary from the CBC. Also available on Google video.

Sodium fluoride, which is really a catch-all term for a variety of chemicals, is "a waste byproduct of the fertilizer and aluminum industry."[7] It has an interesting history of being added to water supplies. One of the first agencies to add sodium fluoride to drinking water was the Nazi Gestapo. The Gestapo, believe it or not, was not concerned with children's dental health. Instead, their goal was to cause sterilization and submissive behavior on the part of the victims in the Nazi concentration camps.[8] Sodium fluoride began to be added to U.S. water supplies in the 1940's. Even while being banned in many parts of Europe; it continues to be used to intentionally contaminate over 60% of municipal drinking water in the United States today. The fluoride content in toothpaste is the reason for the warning label telling you to contact poison control if you happen to swallow it. Sodium fluoride is the primary ingredient in rat poison.[9] Fluoride has never been approved by the FDA.[10] Many dentists who recommend fluoride believe that calcium fluoride is what is being used. However, the chemicals added to drinking water include hydrofluorosilicic acid, which is a classified hazardous waste.[11]

> They call them "wet scrubbers" - the pollution control devices used by the phosphate industry to capture fluoride gases produced in the production of commercial fertilizer. In the past, when the industry let these gases escape, vegetation became scorched, crops destroyed, and cattle crippled. Today, with the development of sophisticated air-pollution control technology, less of the fluoride escapes into the atmosphere, and the type of pollution that

7 "Bizarre Government Coloring Book Pushes Deadly Fluoride for Kids" by Paul Joseph Watson. http://www.prisonplanet.com/articles/june2008/060308_deadly_fluoride.htm

8 *The Crime and Punishment of I.G. Farben* by Joseph Borkin. It is frightening and revealing to study Nazi Germany and compare its programs to those in place the western world today. It does not make sense until you realize that the funding and eugenics ideology comes from the same elite families.

9 "The Five Hidden Dangers in Toothpaste" by Scott Baker. http://www.downwithbasics.com/toothpastedanger.html

10 Ibid: (I am not saying that FDA approval means safety, but lack of approval is certainly a red flag)

11 "The Phosphate Fertilizer Industry: An Environmental Overview" by Michael Connett of the Fluoride Action Network. http://www.fluoridealert.org/phosphate/overview.htm

> threatened the survival of some communities in the 1950s and 60s, is but a thing of the past (at least in the US and other wealthy countries).However, the impacts of the industry's fluoride emissions are still being felt, although more subtly, by millions of people - people who, for the most part, do not live anywhere near a phosphate plant. That is because, after being captured in the scrubbers, the fluoride acid (hydrofluorosilicic acid), a classified hazardous waste, is barreled up and sold, unrefined, to communities across the country. Communities add hydrofluorosilicic acid to their water supplies as the primary fluoride chemical for water fluoridation. Even if you do not live in a community where fluoride is added to water, you'll still be getting a dose of it through cereal, soda, juice, beer and any other processed food and drink manufactured with fluoridated water.[12]

There is a wealth of evidence that water fluoridation has little to no benefit for dental health and is harmful to the body in a plethora of other ways. One of the most harmful effects is IQ reduction, a constant goal for the eugenicists.[13]

> In assessing the potential health effects of fluoride at 2-4 mg/L, the committee found three studies of human populations exposed at those concentrations in drinking water that were useful for informing its assessment of potential neurologic effects. These studies were conducted in different areas of China, where fluoride concentrations ranged from 2.5 to 4 mg/L. Comparisons were made between the IQs of children from those populations with children exposed to lower concentration of fluoride ranging from 0.4 to 1 mg/L. The studies reported that while modal IQ scores were unchanged, the average IQ scores were lower in the more highly exposed children. This was due to fewer children in the high IQ range. While the studies lacked sufficient detail for the committee to fully assess their quality and their relevance to U.S. populations, the consistency of the collective results warrant additional research on the effects of fluoride on intelligence. Investigation of other mental and physiological alterations reported in the case

12 Ibid, I also recommend "Fluoride is Toxic Waste (Literally)" by Chris White on YouTube. http://www.youtube.com/watch?v=LLWk3cBnHOg

13 Positive eugenics is the creation of the "Superman," but those programs are reserved only for the elites themselves. Negative eugenics, the process of dumbing down and thinning out the rest of us is the goal of the programs used on the whole society.

> study literature, including mental confusion and lethargy, should also be investigated.[14]

It is interesting to note that the above study found that fluoride exposure results in "fewer children in the high IQ range." The eugenicists want to keep people dumbed down and "average" to avoid threats to their dominance. Fluoridated water is only one prong of this eugenics attack. There are several other tools used in this chemical attack that we will look at shortly. The overall goal is summed up quite well by Dr. Russell Blaylock in an interview available on YouTube.

> Because of all these different toxins known to affect brain function, we are seeing a society that not only has a lot more people of lower IQ, but a lot fewer people of higher IQ. In other words: a dumbing down, a chemical dumbing down of society. So everyone is sort of mediocre. That leaves them dependent on government, because they can't excel. We have these people of lower IQ who are totally dependent. Then we have this mass of people who are going to believe anything they are told because they can't really think clearly—and very few people of a very high IQ have good cognitive function who can figure this all out. And that is what they want. So you can kind of piece it together as to why they are so insistent in spending so many hundreds of millions of dollars of propaganda money to dumb down society.[15]

Blaylock is referring not only to fluoride but also to chemical food and drink additives such as MSG and aspartame. MSG is a taste enhancer that also stimulates appetite.[16] MSG can cause negative reactions in many areas, including the immune system, the circulatory system, the respiratory system, the digestive system, and the nervous system.[17] MSG can also attack the brain in the following way:

---

14 "2006 National Research Council of the National Academies Report on Fluoride" as posted in "23 Published Studies Report an Association of Reduced IQ With High Fluoride Exposure" http://www.fluoridealert.org/iq.studies.html

15 "Aspartame, MSG, Dumbing Down Society" http://www.youtube.com/watch?v=S8kgJfw699E

16 "What Exactly is MSG?" from an excellent site on the topic, msgtruth.org http://www.msgtruth.org/whatisit.htm

17 "Body Systems Affected by MSG" http://www.msgtruth.org/body.htm

> During periods of hypoglycemia where low blood glucose levels leave the brain with low defenses, or allergy response where the blood vessels become "leaky," MSG may cross the blood brain barrier and damage brain cells by excitatory neurotoxicity. By affecting the pancreas and creating a situation of hypoglycemia, MSG may bring down the brain's barriers, carrying its own key, in a sense, to get to the brain.[18]

"Neurotoxicity," or brain damage, becomes a familiar term when you begin to research the effects of the eugenics programs being carried out through chemical additives and other means.

Another source of neurotoxicity is aspartame, which has a synergistic effect with MSG.[19] Aspartame was refused approval by the FDA for 16 years because studies clearly showed that it caused cancer and brain damage. However, all of that changed because of New World Order ultra-minion Donald Rumsfeld.

> From laboratory testing of the chemical on rats, researchers have discovered that the drug induces brain tumors. On Sept 30, 1980 the Board of Inquiry of the FDA concurred and denied the petition for approval. In 1981, the newly appointed FDA Commissioner, Arthur Hull Hayes, ignored the negative ruling and approved aspartame for dry goods. As recorded in the Congressional Record of 1985, then CEO of Searle Laboratories Donald Rumsfeld said that he would "call in his markers" to get aspartame approved. Rumsfeld was on President Reagan's transition team and a day after taking office appointed Hayes. No FDA Commissioner in the previous sixteen years had allowed aspartame on the market.[20]

Reagan owed Rumsfeld a favor because he had promised him the vice-presidency and then had been forced to take George H.W. Bush instead. Rumsfeld was paid handsomely by Searle—later owned by New World Order mega-corporation Monsanto—with the understanding that he would use his political connections to get a clearly dangerous and poisonous product approved. Rums-

---

18 Ibid

19 Ibid

20 "Donald Rumsfeld and Aspartame" is a great article from newswithviews.com. This article contains references to several of the most respected and well-researched works on aspartame. http://www.newswithviews.com/NWVexclusive/exclusive15.htm

feld has played a pivotal role in everything from arming North Korea with nuclear weapons to deliberately turning the Iraq War into a money-sucking and life destroying quagmire, but pushing through aspartame may have caused even more harm than his other projects.

Aspartame wreaks havoc on the brain in a similar way to MSG.

> Aspartate and glutamate act as neurotransmitters in the brain by facilitating the transmission of information from neuron to neuron. Too much aspartate or glutamate in the brain kills certain neurons by allowing the influx of too much calcium into the cells. This influx triggers excessive amounts of free radicals, which kill the cells. The neural cell damage that can be caused by excessive aspartate and glutamate is why they are referred to as "excitotoxins." They "excite" or stimulate the neural cells to death. The blood brain barrier (BBB), which normally protects the brain from excess glutamate and aspartate as well as toxins, 1) is not fully developed during childhood, 2) does not fully protect all areas of the brain, 3) is damaged by numerous chronic and acute conditions, and 4) allows seepage of excess glutamate and aspartate into the brain even when intact. The excess glutamate and aspartate slowly begin to destroy neurons. The large majority (75 percent or more) of neural cells in a particular area of the brain are killed before any clinical symptoms of a chronic illness are noticed.[21]

The above quote points out an important point about aspartame and MSG. The negative effects on the brain are cumulative; an incredible amount of damage can take place before it is manifested in a specific disease. The health problems linked to aspartame include multiple sclerosis, ALS, memory loss, hearing loss, hormonal problems, epilepsy, Alzheimer's disease, Parkinson's disease, hypoglycemia, AIDS, dementia, brain lesions, and neuroendocrine disorders.[22]

Aspartame is especially damaging to children because the blood brain barrier is not fully developed. It is not surprising, therefore, that many of the thousands of products that contain aspartame are marketed directly at children (candy, soda, chewable vitamins, etc.). The result is exactly what the satanic eugenicists intended—

21 "Aspartame: What You Do not Know Can Hurt You" is an excellent article from mercola.com http://www.mercola.com/article/aspartame/dangers.htm
22 Ibid

many children are turned into brain-damaged entertainment zombies with chronic health problems, who grow up wholly committed to the eugenics state that is hurting them. Arch-eugenicist Bertrand Russell describes the desired effect of the eugenics programs as "the congenital differences between rulers and ruled will increase until they become almost different species. A revolt of the plebs would become as unthinkable as an organized insurrection of sheep against the practice of eating mutton."[23]

Along with adding harmful substances such as aspartame and MSG to our food, the satanic eugenicists have set their sights on changing and damaging food itself through genetic modification. According to the Human Genome Project information page:

> Combining genes from different organisms is known as recombinant DNA technology, and the resulting organism is said to be "genetically modified," "genetically engineered," or "transgenic." GM products (current or those in development) include medicines and vaccines, foods and food ingredients, feeds, and fibers.[24]

GM products are impressively high-tech, but are they safe? We would like to assume that the FDA required extensive, long-term testing on the safety of GM products before approval, but unfortunately that is simply not the case.[25] FDA approval was obtained through industry manipulation and corporate collusion with Monsanto playing a key role.[26] "Scientists were threatened. Evidence was stolen. Data was omitted or distorted. Some regulators even claimed they were offered bribes to approve a GM product.[27] Out of the very few studies that have been conducted, the often frightening findings have been disregarded or white-

23 Bertrand Russell wrote this in *The Impact on Society* in 1953. I quote it here from an excellent article titled "Eugenics Moves to the Twenty-First Century" from Old Thinker News. http://oldthinkernews.com/Articles/oldthinker%20 news/eugenics.htm

24 "Genetically Modified Foods and Organisms" http://www.ornl.gov/sci/techresources/Human_Genome/elsi/gmfood.shtml

25 "Dangers of Genetically Modified Foods" from the Institute for Responsible Technology. http://www.responsibletechnology.org/GMFree/AboutGMFoods/DangersofGMFoods/index.cfm These claims are taken from Jeffrey M. Smith's well-documented book, *Seeds of Deception.*

26 Ibid

27 Ibid

washed. For example, one study tested the effects of a GM crop on a group of forty rats. All the rats developed stomach lesions and seven of the forty died within two weeks. Yet, this was considered enough evidence to show the product was "safe," and it was approved without further tests.[28]

The FDA has adopted the principle of "substantial equivalence," which means that if it still looks like the original product (corn, soybeans, etc), then it will be regulated in the same way.[29] This is patently ridiculous since it effectively ignores the existence of GM products instead of investigating them. Monsanto's lobbying role in this determination as well as their incredible power within the revolving door structure of Washington D.C. politics and big business is clearly shown in the excellent documentary *The World According to Monsanto,* by Marie-Monique Robin.[30]

It is important to realize that the FDA relies on industries to conduct their own safety testing and uses this supposedly reliable data for its evaluations. Many people are aware of the controversy surrounding the rbGH hormone given to milk cows to increase the amount of milk they put out. Looking at the approval process for this product gives us an insight into how this process works.

> Many industry studies appear to be rigged to find no problems. In the case of a genetically engineered bovine growth hormone (rbGH), for example, researchers injected cows with only one forty-seventh the normal dosage before reporting hormone residues in milk. They heated the milk 120 times longer than standard, to report that pasteurization destroys the hormone. They added cows to their study that were pregnant before treatment, to claim that rbGH didn't impede fertility. Cows that fell sick were dropped from

28 Ibid

29 "The Authorisation for the Marketing of GMO's: a Process Closely Managed by Monsanto" from the excellent Combat Monsanto website. http://www.combat-monsanto.co.uk/spip.php?article317

30 *The World According to Monsanto* is available for free on the internet in many places but Robin is certainly a filmmaker that deserves financial support. See www.seedsofdeception.com to order this film and Jeffrey Smith's great book *Seeds of Deception.*

studies altogether.[31]

The FDA is another tentacle of the nanny state. Under the guise of protecting people, it is able to provide cover and protection for eugenicist corporations such as Monsanto. The FDA not only fails in their supposed mission to protect us by allowing incredibly harmful substances such as GM products to be sold; it also has not even required labeling of GM products. In fact, it has banned companies from advertising the fact that their products are non-GMO in some cases. Even foods that are federally approved as "organic" are allowed to contain a sizeable percentage of GM material. It would be much better to have no FDA so that people were at least aware that the foods they consume could very well be dangerous to their health. No one except the GM death-merchants themselves have any reason for opposing clear labeling of GM products. If people want to still buy them, then that is their choice, but people should at least be able to know what they are buying.[32]

The plethora of GM foods that we are consuming either directly or indirectly, either knowingly or unsuspectingly, are having a serious impact on our health. While the convenient lack of studies of the long-term effects of GM food consumption has kept the explicit health effects in doubt for the most part, it is clear from Monsanto's internal studies on rats that GM products damage the immune system and the digestive tract.[33] GMO's have also been linked to the increasing number of people suffering from food allergies, some of them severe and even life-threatening.[34] The satanic eugenicists know that they have unleashed a potential plague on humanity with genetic modification. Because

31 "Dangers of Genetically Modified Foods" from the Institute for Responsible Technology. http://www.responsibletechnology.org/GMFree/AboutGMFoods/DangersofGMFoods/index.cfm These claims are taken from Jeffrey M. Smith's excellent and well-documented book, *Seeds of Deception.*

32 There has been considerable progress made on this front through grassroots action and consumer spending changes, not through government legislation. In fact, the "food safety" programs proposed in Congress in 2009 are designed to benefit New World Order monoliths like Monsanto at the expense of small, independent farmers.

33 "The Damaging Effects of GMO's Revealed" by Dr. Mercola. http://articles.mercola.com/sites/articles/archive/2005/06/11/gmo-effects.aspx

34 "The GMO Controversy" http://www.thenibble.com/reviews/nutri/matter/2006-04.asp

of the propensity of GM products to spread, infect, and take over natural varieties, there is the very real possibility that even if it becomes obvious that GM products are killing us, it may soon be too late to put the genie back in the bottle. The elite are planning for this scenario by creating giant underground "doomsday" seed vaults in various locations including near the Arctic Ocean in Svalbard.[35]

> Bill Gates is investing tens of his millions along with the Rockefeller Foundation, Monsanto Corporation, Syngenta Foundation and the Government of Norway, among others, in what is called the 'doomsday seed bank.'[36]

Whenever arch-eugenicists Bill Gates and the Rockefellers are involved in a program with GMO makers Monsanto and Syngenta, it is hard to be optimistic about its benevolence.

According to Alex Jones, the seed vaults are part of the New World Order's plan to remake civilization in the event that GMO's or some other engineered catastrophe gets out of hand and wipes out most of the population.[37]

Of course, even if the eugenicists are able to remain "in control" of the effects of genetic modification, it is clear from the products that are being developed that genetic modification of food is specifically designed with eugenics in mind.

> A small California biotech company, Epicyte, in 2001 announced the development of genetically engineered corn which contained a spermicide which made the semen of men who ate it sterile. At the time Epicyte had a joint venture agreement to spread its technology with DuPont and Syngenta, two of the sponsors of the Svalbard Doomsday Seed Vault. Epicyte was since acquired by a North Carolina biotech company. Astonishing to learn was that Epicyte had developed its spermicidal GMO corn with research funds from the US Department of Agriculture, the same USDA which, despite worldwide opposition, continued to finance the development of

35 "Doomsday Seed Vault in the Arctic" by F. William Engdahl of Global Research.ca http://www.globalresearch.ca/index.php?context=va&aid=7529

36 Ibid

37 *The Alex Jones Show*, available streaming on the internet from www.infowars.com or in the form of a free podcast, is the best single source of information on the agenda and operations of the New World Order psychopaths.

> Terminator technology, now held by Monsanto.[38]

Isn't it interesting that nanny state structures such as the USDA and FDA, which were ostensibly created in order to "protect consumers," are really involved in funding and covering up eugenicist operations? It is difficult to fight back against Monsanto and its eugenics-based biotech subsidiaries because of the lobbying clout it has in D.C. and even in the court system. Clarence Thomas, for example, is a former Monsanto attorney. These New World Order organizations rely on positive coverage from the corporate media to keep people unaware of their real agenda of eugenics. And, to keep secret the tools they use to accomplish this agenda, such as corn that sterilizes people who eat it. The only solution to resisting the plague of genetic modification of food is making people aware so that their buying habits change and in turn force the corporations to offer natural products in order to stay competitive. The answer is not "food safety" legislation sponsored by spouses of Monsanto executives—like HR 2749, that would make it nearly impossible for small, independent farmers to keep operating while letting the giant corporations continue as they please.[39]

Not content with poisoning our food and water, the eugenics state also attacks the air we breathe. Under the guise of protecting us from global warming, the government has been experimenting with chemtrails for years. While "chemtrails" is the term those opposed to the spraying use, the New World Order labels their programs such things as "geo-engineering," "indirect and semi-direct aerosol spraying," "cloud simulations," "aerosol radiative forcing of climate," and "injecting scatterers into the stratosphere."[40] Whatever term is used, it is not just a "conspiracy theory," it is something that is going on right now and has been since at least the late 1990's. The easiest way to identify chemtrails is to look at airplane contrails in the sky. If they form

---

38 "Doomsday Seed Vault in the Arctic" by F. William Engdahl of Global Research.ca http://www.globalresearch.ca/index.php?context=va&aid=7529

39 "Food Safety Bill HR 2749 Requires Immediate Opposition" by Ethan Huff. http://www.naturalnews.com/026488_food_food_safety_health.html

40 "The Government Is Already 'Geo-Engineering' The Environment" by Paul Joseph Watson. http://www.prisonplanet.com/the-government-is-already-geo-engineering-the-environment.html

and disappear quickly (within a few seconds), then they are not chemtrails. If, on the other hand, they stay in the sky for a long period of time, are formed in a crisscross pattern, and even turn into giant cloud banks, then you know that you are witnessing chemtrails at work.

Most of the government research is ostensibly based on climate. There is hardly consensus in the scientific community that these programs are safe and effective, however. Scientists, such as Alan Robock, have warned that these programs to "combat global warming" could create everything from droughts to floods and have the potential to "create disasters."[41] Weather manipulation is not new and has been used as a weapon as far back as the Vietnam War in the 1960's. Ben Livingston, the "Father of Weather Weapons," admits to leading programs that were capable of modifying hurricanes and greatly increasing or decreasing the rain production of cloud formations.[42]

Malicious weather manipulation is not the only concern when it comes to chemtrails, however. The chemical components of chemtrails have been tested independently on several occasions and several disturbing elements have been discovered.

> Earlier this year, KSLA news investigation found that a substance that fell to earth from a high altitude chemtrail contained high levels of Barium (6.8 ppm) and Lead (8.2 ppm) as well as trace amounts of other chemicals including arsenic, chromium, cadmium, selenium and silver. Of these, all but one are metals, some are toxic while several are rarely or never found in nature.[43]

Barium is found whenever chemtrails are tested. Among other harmful effects, Barium is known to have a negative impact on the human immune system. Through weakening peoples' natural defenses to disease, the satanic eugenicists are able to make their

41 "Rutgers Professor Warns Geoengineering Could 'Create Disasters," Global Famine" by Paul Joseph Watson. http://www.prisonplanet.com/rutgers-professor-warns-geoengineering-could-create-disasters-global-famine.html

42 Information is from an interview with Ben Livingston that is available as part of "The Alex Jones Report November 22, 2005." http://dl.prisonplanet.tv/members/video/221105weeklyreportwmbb.htm

43 "The Government Is Already 'Geo-Engineering' The Environment" by Paul Joseph Watson. http://www.prisonplanet.com/the-government-is-already-geo-engineering-the-environment.html

other programs of poison more effective.

Along with chemtrails, the eugenicists are attacking the human immune system through vaccines. While many people are aware of the link between mercury in vaccines and Autism, most people are not aware of any of the other plethora of dangers injected with the needles of the eugenics state. The corporate media propaganda is that vaccines are safe, effective, and required by law. All three of these claims are easily debunked lies.

Vaccines are not safe or effective. The Vaccine Adverse Event Reporting System receives over "1,000 reports per month of adverse effects from vaccination. Both doctors and the CDC admit that only a fraction of adverse incidents are reported."[44] This also addresses only immediate negative reactions. The long term effects of having known toxic chemicals and carcinogens bypass normal immunological barriers and injected straight in the bloodstream have not been properly researched.

The reason that vaccines are not safe relates directly to the reason they are not effective. The theory behind vaccines is that they incite the same body processes as actually contracting the disease and end up with the same result, immunity. This theory is not borne out by evidence, however, when we consider that diseases that were supposedly eradicated by vaccines, such as Polio, had already declined by 95% before vaccines were introduced and that the rates of disease actually increased with the introduction of vaccines.[45] There are many examples of disease outbreaks affecting children immunized for the disease at the same or greater rate than non-immunized children.[46] While many doctors, health professionals, and parents have seen first-hand the damage caused by vaccines and warned about the dangers, the exact reason for the harmful effects is only in recent years beginning to be fully understood.

No person is a greater opponent of forced immunization than

44 "Three Myths About Vaccines" from Kids Need Options With Vaccines, http://www.know-vaccines.org/3myths.html

45 This information comes from Chris White's excellent website http://www.hendersonvillevaccineawarenessnetwork.com/ which is a great starting place for researching vaccines.

46 Ibid

Dr. Rebecca Carley and consequently few people have been persecuted more by the Rockefeller funded and controlled medical establishment. Her excellent treatise on the mechanism of vaccine damage, "Inoculations: The True Weapons of Mass Destruction" is very important and merits further investigation from the medical research community. In this article, Carley explains how the underlying assumptions about vaccines are tragically wrong.[47]

> What the promoters of vaccination failed to realize is that the respiratory tract of ALL mammals (since animals are just as devastated by these inoculations with disease as are humans) contain secretory IgA (an antibody which initiates the natural God given immune response) within the respiratory tract mucosa. Bypassing this mucosal aspect of the immune system by directly injecting organisms into the bloodstream leads to a corruption in the immune system itself. As a result, the pathogenic viruses or bacteria cannot be eliminated by the immune system and remain in the body, where they will further grow and/or mutate as the individual is exposed to ever more antigens and toxins in the environment which continue to assault the immune system.[48]

In other words, the means of vaccination, injection, prevents the immune system from working properly and leads to a corrupted environment where the immune system is more vulnerable to attack by all the other agents of chemical attack (i.e. aspartame, MSG, HFC, etc.) and more susceptible to cancer and many other diseases. Carley then goes on to describe the long term effects of vaccination on the autoimmune system.

> This hyperactivity of the humoral (antibody producing) pole of the immune system is, in this author's opinion, the sole cause of all autoimmune diseases. The only thing which determines which autoimmune disease you develop is which tissues in your body are attacked by auto-antibodies. If the inside lining of the gastrointestinal tract (the mucosa) is attacked by auto-antibodies you develop leaky gut syndrome (which leads to food allergies when partially digested food particles are released into the bloodstream, are recognized as antigens foreign to the body, and elicit an antibody response against

47 "Inoculations: The Real Weapons of Mass Destruction" by Rebecca Carley, M.D. http://www.infowars.com/innoculations-the-true-weapons-of-mass-destruction/
48 Ibid

those food particles that becomes heightened every time that same food is eaten and released into the bloodstream partially digested again). Crohn's disease and colitis are also caused by auto-antibody attack on the mucosa of the GI tract itself. If the islet (insulin producing) cells of the pancreas are attacked by auto-antibodies, you develop insulin dependent (juvenile) diabetes. If the respiratory mucosa is attacked by auto-antibodies, you develop "leaky lung" syndrome where, just as with leaky gut, antigens recognized as foreign to the body which are inhaled are able to traverse the lining of the respiratory tract, causing the creation of antibodies against those antigens (usually dust, mold, pet or pollen antigens). When these substances are inhaled again, the allergic response producing constriction of the bronchioles is called asthma. If the components of the articular surface of the joints are attacked by auto-antibodies, you develop rheumatoid (or juvenile) arthritis.

If the skin is attacked, you develop "leaky skin" syndrome, where contact antigens which could not otherwise traverse the skin are allowed in, leading to skin allergies to contact antigens. Additionally, depending on which level of the skin is attacked by auto-antibodies, (i.e., the epidermis or dermis), you develop eczema, psoriasis or scleroderma. If the kidney tissue is attacked by auto-antibodies, you develop one of the many types of nephritis, depending on which component of renal tissue is attacked (for example, with glomerulonephritis, the basement membrane of the glomerular apparatus within the kidney (which filters blood to form urine) is attacked by auto-antibodies, thus allowing protein to escape from the serum into the urine).

If you develop auto-antibodies against thyroid gland tissue, you develop Grave's disease. If you develop auto-antibodies against the tissue of the thymus gland (which is crucial in T cell production and function), you develop myasthenia gravis. If you develop auto-antibodies against the very DNA in the nucleus of all cells, you develop systemic Lupus (thus, the potential autoimmune potential of DNA vaccines being developed now is self evident; worse yet, DNA components from these vaccines can be incorporated into your DNA, leading to actual genetic changes which could cause extinction of all (vaccinated) life on the Earth). And on, and on, and on.

The brain and spinal cord can also be attacked with auto-antibodies (which this author refers to as vaccine induced encephalitis), leading to a variety of neurological diseases. The most severe of these, leading to death, are sudden infant death syndrome (SIDS) and most cases of "shaken baby syndrome". If components of the myelin sheath (the insulating covering of nerve fibers which allows

> proper nerve conduction) or the actual neurofilaments themselves are attacked by auto-antibodies, the resultant condition is determined solely by the location of the damage done. Such neurological conditions include but are not limited to minimal brain dysfunction, ADD/ADHD, learning disabilities, mental retardation, criminal behavior, the spectrum of pervasive developmental disorders (including autism), multiple sclerosis, Parkinson's, Lou Gehrig's disease, Guillen Barre,, seizure disorders, etc., etc. etc. (Please note that other toxins are also sometimes involved, such as: aspartame, Lyme's and mercury in cases of MS; aspartame in seizures; or pesticides in cases of Parkinson's).[49]

If Dr. Carley is correct, then it is clear that vaccination is a key component to the New World Order eugenics state agenda. Not only does it fit with the genocidal goals of the elite to reduce population by at least 80%, but it also ensures a compliant mass of people to govern. Sick people have their wealth and energy sucked out of them by the New World Order and it is hard for them to fight back.

There is no state in the United States where vaccination is required by law. The illusion that refusing to be vaccinated is illegal has been created through color of law tricks and corporate media complicity. For example, you may hear on the news that your children must be vaccinated before they can attend school. The school, at the urging and financial incentivizing of the federal or state government, makes proof of vaccination "mandatory" for students attending school. If students and their parents do not provide proof of vaccination, the student is told they cannot attend school. If the student still is not vaccinated, truancy laws activate and the students and/or parents can get in legal trouble.[50]

If you or someone you love must attend the government training camp known as the public school (a bad idea for many reasons), there are several ways to avoid the mandatory vaccine requirement. All states offer a waiver form that is available for health, religious, and sometimes philosophical reasons. Of course, filling out a waiver should not be required for something that is not illegal in the first place, but it is an option. There are also certain groups of

49 Ibid

50 Alex Jones has gone over this New World Order trick many times on *The Alex Jones Show*.

students (i.e. homeless students), for whom the usual paperwork is not required. However, having your child claim to be homeless introduces many other nanny state programs that it is certainly a good idea to stay far away from. The best option, of course, is to avoid vaccination and public education altogether.

In this chapter, we have taken a brief glance at several programs within the overall framework of the eugenics wars. Unfortunately, many books can and have been written on each of these areas. There are also many programs that I have not covered at all. If you cannot believe that things are really this bad or that they are being done intentionally, I strongly encourage you to do your own research. Just because you and I are not psychopathic or sociopathic control freaks does not mean that they do not exist. And, it does not mean they are not pulling the strings of politicians, bureaucrats, doctors, etc, from behind the curtain at the behest of the ultimate control freak and lover of death and deception, Satan himself. In the next chapter we will look behind the visible government to a deeper layer of the New World Order system, the invisible government of secret societies and political think tanks.

## Chapter 10

# Satan's Strings: Secret Societies and Their Foundation Funding

Secret societies and other versions of the power behind the throne are nothing new in history. No monarch ever gained and maintained control without the support of other wealthy and powerful individuals. Some secret societies wield spiritual as well as political power through closely guarding and passing down occult knowledge. This knowledge came from evil angelic forces to everyone from Nimrod and the Babylonian sun cults to the Egyptians and the Freemasons, the Illuminati, and their collective satanic incarnations today. In this chapter, we will focus on modern forms of the satanic secret societies; in particular, how they wield political power, how they are organized, and how they are linked to Luciferianism and Satan worship through rituals and ceremonies.

Many secret societies are openly acknowledged organizations; such as the Trilateral Commission, Council on Foreign Relations, Freemasons, Skull and Bones, etc. The real purpose, agenda, and reach of power of these organizations are far beyond what is presented in the corporate media, however. Other groups are so secretive that their very existence is denied by the corporate media—such as the Illuminati or Bilderberg Group. When forced to admit that these groups exist, the corporate media usually follow a couple of scripted lies to keep people in the dark: 1) "okay that group used to exist but it doesn't anymore and everything's fine," or 2) "yes they exist but they have no real power and they love you anyway." These whitewashing distortions are presented by laughing anchors or through books that supposedly investigate these groups.[1]

1 Examples include CNN's October 2009 piece on Freemasonry or any of Alexandra Robbins' books.

Alternative media sources have often pointed to an overrepresentation of secret society members in Presidential Administrations, as well as the non-coverage of these affiliations by the corporate media, as evidence that the "invisible" government wields far more power than we might expect. The Trilateral Commission, formed in 1973 by David Rockefeller, has had an extensive presence in U.S. administrations as well as the political power structure of Europe and Asia.[2] Despite having a "ceiling" of 87 members from the U.S. at any one time,[3] President Obama appointed eleven of those 87 Trilateral members to high level cabinet positions within two weeks of taking office.[4] Specifically, those appointments were Secretary of Treasury Timothy Geithner, Ambassador to the U.N. Susan Rice, National Security Advisor Gen. James L. Jones, Deputy National Security Advisory Thomas Donilon, Chairman of the Economic Recovery Committee Paul Volker, Director of National Intelligence Admiral Dennis C. Blair, Assistant Secretary of State, Asia and Pacific Kurt M. Campbell, Deputy Secretary of State James Steinberg, and State Department Special Envoys Richard Haass, Dennis Ross, and Richard Holbrooke.[5] The Obama Administration is no different from other administrations dating back to the administration of Jimmy Carter, himself a Trilateral Commission member and Brzezinski protégé. Notice that these appointments are focused on foreign policy and the financial system. These are the two areas that are in many ways the most crucial, and not coincidentally they are the ones most controlled by secret society interests. They are also two of the areas where regardless of whether a Democrat or Republican is elected; the same policies are carried forward.[6]

Many of the Trilateral Commission members are also members of the Council on Foreign Relations (a much larger organization), and some are also members of the Bilderberg Group.

2 See the Trilateral Commission's own website at www.trilateral.org

3 Ibid

4 "Obama: Trilateral Commission Endgame" by Patrick Wood on The August Review website, which is an excellent research source. http://www.augustreview.com/news_commentary/trilateral_commission/obama:_trilateral_commission_endgame_20090127110/

5 Ibid

6 Notice, for example, that Obama retained Secretary of Defense Robert Gates and re-appointed Ben Bernanke as Federal Reserve Chairman.

There has been a lot of great research in this area but a good place to start is Alex Jones' film *The Obama Deception*, which lists Obama's key cabinet members and their affiliations with those three elite organizations.[7] The fact that power positions in the visible government are dominated by members of these organizations is easy to verify via research. More controversial is the issue of whether these organizations have a malicious agenda, and if they have the means of pushing that agenda through in the visible government.

The purposes of the Trilateral Commission, CFR, and the Bilderberg Group are strikingly similar. The Trilateral Commission website states their purpose is "to foster closer cooperation among these core democratic industrialized areas of the world with shared leadership responsibilities in the wider international system."[8] What this means, of course, is the dissolution of a system of independent and sovereign nations in favor of supranational power wielded by organizations such as the Trilateral Commission.

> At a deeper level, there was a sense that the United States was no longer in such a singular leadership position as it had been in earlier post-World War II years, and that a more shared form of leadership—including Europe and Japan in particular—would be needed for the international system to navigate successfully the major challenges of the coming years. The "growing interdependence" that so impressed the founders of the Trilateral Commission in the early 1970s has deepened into "globalization." That interdependence also has ensured that the current financial crisis has been felt in every nation and region.[9]

Compare the above sentiments with the goal of the Council on Foreign Relations according to Carroll Quigley, a prominent establishment historian at Georgetown University, Bill Clinton's mentor, and author of *Tragedy and Hope*. "The CFR is the American Branch of a society which originated in England, and which believes that national boundaries should be obliterated, and a one-

7 *The Obama Deception* is available at infowars.com or viewable for free on YouTube. http://www.youtube.com/watch?v=eAaQNACwaLw

8 http://www.trilateral.org/about.htm

9 Ibid

world rule established."[10] The Bilderberg Group focuses on improving the relationship between Europe and the United States as well as the creation and expansion of what is now known as the European Union.[11] "Interdependence," "cooperation," "shared responsibility," "international crisis," "new economic order," and "global governance" are just some of the buzzwords that these three organizations are constantly using in their publications and in the speeches of their many puppet politicians. What it comes down to, of course, is the establishment of world government. For this cause, crises such as flu pandemics are manufactured, entire economies are deliberately imploded, false flag terrorist attacks are carried out, imaginary threats to our existence such as global warming are hyped incessantly, and any nation who tries to remain independent is labeled a rogue state and either demolished militarily or starved into submission by sanctions.

On one level, these organizations share a common purpose because it is the purpose of their founders (mainly Rothschilds, Rockefellers, Carnegie, etc.) to increase their power and control to a world-wide spectrum. I agree with Russ Dizdar, however, that there is a deeper level to this agenda. There is a "spirit of globalism" that comes from Satan and his demonic minions that drives the New World Order in their obsessive quest for world government.[12] They are building towards the time that is described in Revelation 17:12-14.

> The ten horns which you saw are ten kings who have received no kingdom as yet, but they receive authority for one hour as kings with the beast. These are of one mind, and they will give their power and authority to the beast. These will make war with the Lamb, and the Lamb will overcome them, for He is Lord of lords and King of kings; and those who are with him are called, chosen, and faithful.[13]

---

10 http://www.councilonforeignrelations.net/

11 See "The Bilderberg Group and the Project of European Unification" by Professor Mike Peters at Bilderberg.org http://www.bilderberg.org/bildhist.htm#The

12 Russ Dizdar is someone whom I very much trust regarding issues of spiritual warfare. Check out his book *The Black Awakening* and his website www.shatterthedarkness.net

13 Revelation 17: 12-14 (I am not claiming this will happen in the immediate future, but I do think it is clear that Satan is preparing his minions and systems to deceive people and to fight against Jesus Christ and his followers.)

It would behoove us to notice that amidst all the apparent strife of the political and economic systems of the world, there is certainly a powerful and cohesive drive toward a centralized New World Order.

On the political level, policies are disseminated and put into practice through organizations like the CFR and its puppet politicians. Nearly every piece of legislation is written by corporate special interest groups. Moreover, the major pieces of legislation on foreign policy, health care, carbon taxes, etc, are prepared by members of the Council on Foreign Relations. It is the job of those at the CFR and affiliated think tanks to come up with disguises and justifications for the systems that will allow the breaking down of U.S. sovereignty and individual freedom: all for the sake of building the world government and New World Order. It is these disguises and justifications, not the real agenda, that is "debated" on television and in the halls of congress. Along with fake philosophical support, these pieces of legislation are pushed through by the tried and true methods of blackmailing and bribing members of the House and Senate. Dig into the background of anyone from the level of Committee Chairman on up. You will find out why politicians are beholden to behind the scenes forces rather than just working for the good of the people. This is especially true, again, in the areas of finance and foreign policy. Is it any wonder, then, that the head of the Banking Committee is a man like Barney Frank?[14]

Organizations such as the CFR are clearly the conduit from which the agenda of the elite: globalization, is sold to the politicians, the media, and indirectly to the public. However, a deeper question is how exactly is the satanic agenda imprinted on the hearts and minds of the elite so universally and completely? The answer to this is also related to secret societies, but this time of a more spiritual variety. Groups such as the Bohemian Club of Bohemian Grove, Skull and Bones, and various other occult

14 As of 2009—I do not want to get into Barney Frank's sordid past, but any amount of research shows that his is a background full of blackmail material. In fact, when you see a politician get burned in the media, it is not because they are dirtier than the others. It usually means they tried to do something good for the people and against the banks. See "Governors Discover Resisting the Fed has Consequences" by Kevin Jones. http://www.infowars.com/governors-discover-resisting-the-fed-has-consequences/

groups feature both extremely powerful members and extremely depraved practices.

The organization of many of these societies is very similar. This is further evidence, along with common founders and a common agenda, that there is a common hand directing these organizations from behind the scenes. The most common structure of these organizations is severely hierarchical. The true scope of the society's agenda is visible only to the select few at the top of the pyramid. The bottom layers are the most public and the most populated. Most Freemasons, for example, are in the first three degrees—the Blue Lodge, and are purposefully misled as to the meaning of the ceremonies they are a part of and the symbols of the lodge.[15] Most of the CFR's 4,000 plus members are not part of setting the agenda, but are just trying to pad their networking and political credentials. Most attendees to the Bohemian Grove are corporate chieftains who may not be practicing occultists in their daily lives.

The middle layers of these organizations are given specialized and compartmentalized knowledge that helps them carry out specific tasks. A member may begin to see some evil elements at this point, but either gullibly believes it is "for the greater good" or is easily corrupted by promises of increased power and wealth. Members at these levels are fed different layers of propaganda and are led to believe they are initiated into the real agenda. When, in fact, they are still being deceived. In fact, it is the job of many of the members of these organizations to come up with reasons or excuses for pieces of the agenda which they may even genuinely believe themselves. Most politicians fall into this category and are paid to sell the false explanations such as "national security," "fighting terrorism," "expanding healthcare to all," "saving the environment," etc, to the people they supposedly represent.

The top layers of these organizations, while usually hidden far from view, share an uncanny commonality of purpose. This purpose is always the accumulation and consolidation of power.

15 For an excellent resource that covers many more secret societies and associated conspiracies than I cover here, see Jim Marrs' book *Rule by Secrecy*. The last part of the book is mostly bogus, but the sections on the organizations I mention in this book are helpful.

Another commonality is the prevalence of Luciferians and occultists at this level of many of the organizations. The average Freemason would be shocked to learn that the "harmless" rituals he has taken part in at his local lodge are merely imitations of and initiations into shocking satanic rituals that occur at the highest levels. These rituals are performed by the Freemasons, the Bohemian Grove members, the Skull and Bones members and the Illuminati. They involve the worship of pagan gods and of Satan himself, and provide the real power source and agenda behind the invisible government structure.[16]

At the Bohemian Grove, thousands of wealthy businessmen and political leaders, including Presidents George W. Bush, Bill Clinton, George H.W. Bush, Ronald Reagan, Richard Nixon, and New World Order honchos like Henry Kissinger gather to "stand naked against the redwood trees,"[17] participate in homosexual orgies,[18] and most disturbingly of all, to take part in a pagan ritual called the Cremation of Care. This ritual can be traced back to ancient druidic and even Babylonian roots. It involves the mock human sacrifice of an innocent victim to a giant stone idol in the shape of an owl that the Bohemian Grove members call Moloch.[19] This is carried out by a number of torch bearing men in black druidic robes with KKK-style headwear. This ritual is a

16 See http://www.shatterthedarkness.net/ for details on satanic ritual abuse and the spiritual motivation for it. The fact that these rituals take place in these various organizations is verifiable to a certain extent by the sheer number of entries written about them on the Internet, although first hand accounts are not always reliable. Cathy O'Brien is one former victim of these sorts of atrocities and I believe she is telling the truth about her experiences. http://www.trance-formation.com/ I also recommend Mark Dice's books *The Resistance Manifesto* and *Illuminati: Facts and Fiction* available at http://www.theresistancemanifesto.com/

17 Bill Clinton's assessment of Bohemian Grove (where he denies attending) is viewable on a video titled "Clinton Lies About Bohemian Grove." http://www.youtube.com/watch?v=kP3cQDitQEU&feature=related

18 Richard Nixon called it "the most faggy goddamned thing you could ever imagine" and the New York Post reported in 2004 that gay porn star Chad Savage had been hired to "service" Bohemians during the event. See "2008 Bohemian Grove Guest List Obtained by 9/11 Truth Activists" by Steve Watson and Paul Watson. http://www.infowars.com/2008-bohemian-grove-guest-list-obtained-by-911-truth-activists-2/

19 See the Bible passages specifically addressing the worship of Moloch: Acts 7:43 and Jeremiah 25:9-12.

blasphemous counterfeit and reversal of Jesus Christ's death on the cross because the ritual slaying of the innocent victim is supposed to satisfy "Care," or the men's consciences. This is done so that they are free to fully embrace their evil desires without any moral compunction. The owl itself is a common occult symbol with several different meanings that pagan societies have attached to it through the years—death, wisdom, evil omen, etc, and is now the logo of the Bohemian Club.[20] It may be hard to believe that America's supposedly "conservative Christian" political leaders would participate in this occult ceremony, but the Cremation of Care was captured by courageous independent film maker Alex Jones in *Dark Secrets: Inside Bohemian Grove.*[21]

The Illuminati is a murky organization that includes well-documented incarnations, many rumors, people on the Internet who claim to be "Illuminati defectors," blatant disinformation, and endless combinations of the above. Mark Dice has done extensive research to try and determine what is true and what is a lie and he discloses this extensive research in his book, *Illuminati: Facts and Fiction.*[22] In my own research, I have found that most "defectors" are quite unreliable as far as finding out how the Illuminati operate. This is because the defectors are either deliberately spreading disinformation, or are themselves deceived.

I do believe, however, that some former victims of mind control and satanic ritual abuse are telling the truth about their experiences. Many of these individuals connect these experiences to individuals that are part of what they call the Illuminati, as well as other NWO organizations such as Bohemian Grove. Government programs such as MK-ULTRA used satanic ritual abuse to inflict such pain on children that they were able to create split personalities. These split personalities could then be programmed to perform in whatever way the handlers desired. Two of the most common "programs" that were created were one for the creation

20 The owl is also hidden on the back of the dollar bill and some of the streets of Washington D.C. around the capitol have been designed in the shape of an owl. See Chris Pinto's excellent films *Riddles in Stone* and *Secrets of the Dollar Bill.*

21 This film is available from www.infowars.com, by subscribing to www.prisonplanet.tv , or for free in lower quality on Google video. http://video.google.com/videoplay?docid=-8209591705734983

22 Mark's books and other materials are available at http://www.theresistancemanifesto.com/

of assassins and one for sex slaves. The programmed personalities can sit in a dormant state while the person lives a normal life until triggered to perform something that the handler commands.

Two former mind-controlled sex slaves that have escaped and successfully been de-programmed are Cathy O'Brien and Brice Taylor. Both have written books about their respective ordeals.[23] Their experiences are horrifying, and provide the stark realization that there is deep satanic evil at work in the world today. One of the "assassin" program individuals who have come forward is Robert Duncan O'Finioan. He underwent training to create a similar type of assassin to the "Jason Bourne" character depicted in the *Bourne Identity* and subsequent films.[24]

Along with satanic ritual abuse-based mind control, there are a number of other programs that the Illuminati use to train their members and to ensure that their secrets are secure. Some of these methods were revealed by one of the few trustworthy defectors, a woman who goes by the name Svali, in her article "How the Cult Programs People."[25] Svali claims that programming focuses on five major areas: training to be silent, training to be strong, training to be loyal, training for jobs in the group, and spiritual training.[26]

> The first category, training to be silent, begins at a very young age, frequently preverbal. This is accomplished in several ways, depending upon the child and the trainer, and can include:
>
> Being asked after a ceremony what the child saw and heard. The very young child may just say "bad things", and is punished severely and brutally, and told that no, they didn't really see those things. This is repeated at frequent intervals, until the child learns to block the ceremonies. Often, a "protector" or "guardian" alter will be created from the abuse, whose job is to ensure that the child will

23 Information about these books is found in an article about them by Henry Makow called "Illuminati Sex-Slaves Paint Horrifying Picture." http://www.the7thfire.com/new_world_order/illuminati/Henry_Makow/illuminati_sex_slaves.htm

24 Chris White conducted an extensive interview with O'Finioan which is available in his Nowhere to Run podcast from September 11, 2007. O'Finioan has also recounted his experience in *Innocence Turned Deadly* which is available at http://www.wintersteel.com/RobertDuncanOFinioan.html

25 "How the Cult Programs People" is available at http://www.suite101.com/article.cfm/ritual_abuse/41699

26 Ibid

> not remember what is seen. This protector is told that if the child does remember, brutal punishment will follow.
>
> Another method involves electro-shocking the child, and placing them into a deep hypnotic trance, where they are told that they will not remember what they have seen or heard, that it is all "just a bad dream." The child WANTS to forget, and will be eager to agree.
>
> Psychological torture may be used: mock burials, being placed in cages, abandonment, being hung over a bridge, with the child later being "rescued" and told that if they ever tell, they will be returned to the punishment.
>
> Being forced to watch mock or real punishment or killing of a traitor who "told". When I was four years old, I was forced to watch a woman be skinned alive. Her crime: she disclosed to an outside person "family business". Talking to those outside the group is considered one of the worst crimes or betrayals a person can commit. A "traitor's death" is one of the most horrifying imaginable, and will vary from crucifixion upside down, to other gruesome scenarios. Young children do not forget seeing these things, and they become convinced that not disclosing is the safest way to continue living.
>
> These set ups are done to ensure that a young child will not disclose the criminal activities that they are seeing in the course of group activities, or even as an adult, when they are more actively engaged in them.
>
> Another set up also is frequently done: The "no one will believe you scenario" (this is usually done with school age children). The child is told repeatedly that even if they DO disclose that no one will believe them. The child is taken by a mental hospital, or even taken to visit an inmate briefly. Later, the child is told that people who disclose are considered "crazy" and sent to institutions, where they are punished severely and can never leave. These lies are told to reinforce once again the importance of not telling.[27]

Unfortunately, there is a wealth of horrific stories out there to validate what Svali is writing about. The Illuminati is really just a fancy name for a giant hereditary and hierarchical satanic cult whose tentacles spread throughout the modern world. It is certainly easier to deny this reality than it is to face it. However, I believe it is crucial for Christians to understand that we are involved in a war with an evil and hideous strength.

Skull and Bones, the exclusive Yale secret society that was founded as an American chapter to a German secret society,

27 Ibid

is considered by some to be the controlling force behind the CFR.[28] Skull and Bones has been credited for the creation of the CIA, which seems appropriate because it was created out of profits from the dealing of opium.[29] Skull and Bones has also been rumored to have been the driving force behind the decision to drop the atomic bomb, while Bohemian Grove brags about being the place where the scheme for the Manhattan Project was first hatched.[30] All of this becomes particularly disturbing when we consider the rituals that take place in the Skull and Bones "Tomb."

> "The Hangman equals death, The Devil equals death, Death equals death!" It's weird to think that the two men who are now contesting the most powerful job in world politics, both apparently went through an occult ritual that involved dressing-up and chanting the words above, prostrate in front of a fellow student wielding a butchers' knife and dressed in animal skin.[31]

The two men are of course George W. Bush, and his cousin John Kerry. Other rituals include the drinking of "blood" from a skull-shaped "Yorick" to seal membership and laying naked in a coffin while recounting sexual secrets.[32] Despite corporate media attempts at whitewashing and minimizing the impact of Skull and Bones, it is clear that this secret society has influenced America and that the satanic rituals and love of death have certainly impacted the political elites that were a part of it.

---

28 *Rule by Secrecy* by Jim Marrs. Marrs attributes this claim to Anthony C. Sutton on page 90.

29 The CIA deals drugs and launders the money for big banks. This has been exposed several times but not to a great enough extent where their operations actually get shut down or properly investigated. One example of CIA involvement in the drug trade is found here http://www.infowars.com/update-on-cia-drug-plane-owned-by-%e2%80%9cdonna-blue-aircraft-inc%e2%80%9d/

30 See *Skull and Bones: The Order of Death* by Alex Jones. http://video.google.com/videosearch?q=Skull+and+Bones+&hl=en&emb=0&aq=f#

31 "Skeleton Key to the White House" by Matthew Wells for the London Guardian (February 24, 2004) http://www.prisonplanet.com/240204_skeleton_key_to_the_whitehouse.html

32 "Structures of Power, Secrets, and Publishing" by David L. Beck of the Mercury News. http://www.prisonplanet.com/structures_of_power_secrets_and_publishing.html , http://www.theforbiddenknowledge.com/hardtruth/more_skull_and_bones.htm

The Freemasons are known to be frequent perpetrators of satanic ritual abuse.[33] The Freemasons trace their secret knowledge of architecture back to Egypt and have had their guild "Illuminated," which formed one of the links between ancient and modern secret societies.[34] The Freemasons' political power has often been discussed by independent researchers. For example, fourteen U.S. Presidents have been known Freemasons, with Harry S. Truman, dropper of the atomic bomb, one of the most enthusiastic and involved masons.[35]

Neither the political power nor the satanic ritual abuse is surprising when we consider that at its highest levels, Freemasonry teaches the worship of Lucifer. Two of Freemasonry's most influential leaders have been Manly P. Hall and Albert Pike.

> When the Mason learns that the key to the warrior on the block is the proper application of the dynamo of living power, he has learned the mystery of his Craft. The seething energies of Lucifer are in his hands, and before he may step onward and upward, he must prove his ability to properly apply energy.[36]
>
> If Lucifer were not God, would Adonay whose deeds prove his cruelty, perfidy, and hatred of man, barbarism and repulsion for science, would Adonay and his priests, calumniate him?
>
> Yes, Lucifer is God, and unfortunately Adonay is also God. For the eternal law is that there is no light without shade, no beauty without ugliness, no white without black, for the absolute can only exist as two Gods: darkness being necessary to light to serve as its

33 Please see "Freemasonry and Satanic Ritual Abuse" by a survivor named Neal. The article contains quotes from Christian counselors around the country who frequently have patients that were the victims of satanic Freemasons. http://www.the7thfire.com/new_world_order/Freemasonry/freemasonry_and_satanic_ritual_abuse.htm

34 *Rule by Secrecy* by Jim Marrs, pp. 242-243.

35 "Masonic and Anti-Masonic Presidents of the United States" http://www.bessel.org/presmas.htm Research that points to one particular group always comes up short. The reality is that all of these different secret societies are at their core part of the same satanic cult.

36 Quote from Manly P. Hall in *The Lost Keys of Freemasonry*, cited from "Masonry Proven Conclusively to be Worship of Lucifer, Satan" by Cutting Edge Ministries. http://www.cuttingedge.org/free11.html This is a thorough and well-documented article that I recommend to anyone with questions on this issue.

> foil as the pedestal is necessary to the statue, and the brake to the locomotive.[37]

According to Freemasonry, Lucifer is the "good" god of light and knowledge, while "Adonay" is the cruel and vengeful God whom the foolish Christians and Jews worship. The heart of Luciferian doctrine is the elevation of man to godhood, the elevation of Lucifer to the level of God, and the subjugation of Jesus Christ to something less than the rightful ruler of the universe and of all mankind. While there are hundreds of different flavors in our Satan-drenched media and culture, the message of salvation through means other than the blood of Jesus Christ is the one message that Lucifer is desperately trying to get all men to accept. It is only when Jesus Christ regenerates our hearts that we can be saved and can learn to see Satan's lies for what they are.

What is the ultimate purpose of the satanic rituals within secret societies? While there are multiple purposes, it seems quite unlikely that such a huge emphasis would be put on these rituals—and such risks taken by individuals participating in them, if there was not a strong belief that these rituals bring real power to those that practice them. This is ridiculous from the modern materialistic view of the world. However, these rituals make perfect sense if we view the world through the lens of spiritual warfare. Satan's minions receive real power from the blood of their ritual sacrifices and other evil deeds. In spite of this, no satanic power can stand against the power of the true blood sacrifice of Jesus Christ's crucifixion and the death-conquering power of His resurrection.

Satan's only chance is to distract people from reality with constant diversions, enticements, and temptations in the physical world. Satan's only opportunity for success is to operate in secret and hope that his operations are not exposed. Satan must hide the truth; not only from Christians and the general public, but also from his own minions. He knows that his angelic and demonic forces are no match for even the name of Jesus Christ.[38]

---

37 Albert Pike quote originally from *Morals and Dogma*, cited here from "Quotations Written by High Level Masons Praising Lucifer" http://www.freemasonrywatch.org/luciferquotes.html

38 Russ Dizdar's work at www.shatterthedarkness.net is an excellent resource for understanding the spiritual war that is taking place and how important the role of prayer is in the battle.

## Chapter 11

# False Flag Terrorism

"False flag," and "inside job," are terms that have only recently been added to the common nomenclature—thanks in large part to scrutiny regarding the events of 9/11. The term false flag refers to an event where the real perpetrators and planners of an act of violence remain hidden while a patsy is quickly identified as the culprit. The motive behind false flag attacks is pretty simple: to demonize political opponents while simultaneously galvanizing political support both for the attacked group and from the attacked group.

The success of false flag attacks depends on keeping the identity of the true perpetrators secret. So it is no surprise that mainstream history books record only a small percentage of these events and stick mainly to the official version of events. Even with this inherent underreporting, however, there are many well known occurrences of false flag attacks throughout history.

Nero, whether he started the fire or not, blamed the burning of Rome on Christians in order to give his subjects an enemy and to deflect criticism and accusations from himself and his ambitiously-selfish building plans.

Most historians now believe that Hitler carried out at least two false flag attacks. The first was the burning of the Reichstag—where Hitler had conveniently chosen not to locate his personal office—in 1933. The Reichstag fire aided Hitler's ascendancy, led to new legislation similar to America's Patriot Act, and led to a further consolidation and increased intensity of state power. Hitler's second false flag attack occurred in 1939. Hitler had some German prisoners dressed up as Polish soldiers, taken out to the

Gleiwitz radio station, and machine gunned to death. Then, some German soldiers shouted threats to the German people over the radio and insisted that Poland was going to attack. It didn't matter that Poland was dwarfed by Germany's military strength and would never have considered an invasion. What mattered was Hitler was able to convince the German people that they had been attacked and that they were justified in fighting back against their evil Polish invaders by invading Poland.

This strategy for energizing the civilian population was admitted by Herman Goering a few days before his scheduled execution. After admitting that the people as a whole do not want war, Goering wrote the following:

> It is the leaders of the country who determine the policy and it is always a simple matter to drag the people along, whether it is a democracy or a fascist dictatorship or a Parliament or a Communist dictatorship. ... All you have to do is tell them they are being attacked and denounce the pacifists for lack of patriotism and exposing the country to danger.[1]

Another of the Axis powers, Japan, blew up its own railway tracks and blamed Chinese soldiers as the pretext for invading Manchuria in 1931. This "Mukden incident" initiated the Pacific theater of WWII.

Most Christians do not have a hard time believing that Imperial Japan, Nero, and Hitler were each capable of carrying out a false flag attack, but surely that would never happen in America, right?

Unfortunately, America has a long history of lying and staging events as an excuse for war. David Ray Griffin cites some of the lies that Americans have been fed in order to incite war support.

> The United States itself has used lies to start many wars: the Mexican-American war, based on President Polk's false claim that Mexico had "shed American blood on the American soil"; the Spanish-American war, started on the basis of the false claim that Spain had sunk the U.S. battleship Maine; the war in the Philippines, based on

1 Herman Goering, founder of the infamous Gestapo. http://www.snopes.com/quotes/goering.asp

> the false claim that Filipinos had fired first; and the full-scale part of the Vietnam war, based on the Tonkin Gulf hoax.[2]

The infamous attack on the U.S.S. Liberty was a false flag attack that failed in its attempt to provide a pretext for the U.S.A. and Israel to attack Egypt. Israeli pilots identified the Liberty as an American ship and at first refused to fire, but were threatened with court martial if they didn't follow orders.[3] President Lyndon B. Johnson recalled American ships en-route to aid the Liberty. Johnson told Admiral Geiss, "I want that ship going to the goddamned bottom. No help. Recall the wings."[4]

Operation Northwoods is the name of a government plan to carry out false flag attacks including the fake hijacking of aircraft to gain the support of Americans for the invasion of Cuba.[5] President Kennedy rejected the plan after it had already been approved by the Joint Chiefs. A more recent proposal to commit false flag attacks to justify war with Iran was uncovered by Seymour Hersh.[6] Hersh related the contents of a meeting Vice President Dick Cheney held with other neocons.

> "There was a dozen ideas proffered about how to trigger a war," Hersh explains. "The one that interested me the most was why do not we build — we in our shipyard — build four or five boats that look like Iranian PT boats. Put Navy seals on them with a lot of

---

2 David Ray Griffin, *The New Pearl Harbor Revisited*. I highly recommend all of Griffin's books on the subject of 9/11. He does a great job of putting together the highest quality evidence from a wide-variety of sources.

3 "New Revelations in Attack on American Spy Ship" by John Crewdson in the Baltimore Sun. http://www.baltimoresun.com/news/world/chi-liberty_tuesoct02%2C0%2C6015776.story, also check out "So Who's Afraid of the Israel Lobby" by former CIA analyst Ray McGovern which includes a lot of material on the Liberty http://prisonplanet.com/articles/october2007/071007Lobby.htm

4 *Terrorstorm: A History of Government Sponsored Terror* by Alex Jones. This is an excellent and eye-opening documentary that includes historical examples of false flag terror as well as in-depth analysis of the 9/11 attacks. http://video.google.com/videoplay?docid=-5948263607579389947&ei=NSV0SpSLO4GKqAOL_tTOBQ&q=Terrorstorm

5 "Pentagon Proposed Pretexts for the Invasion of Cuba in 1962" from the George Washington University national security archive. http://www.gwu.edu/~nsarchiv/news/20010430/

6 "Preparing the Battlefield" by Seymour Hersh in the New Yorker Magazine. http://www.newyorker.com/reporting/2008/07/07/080707fa_fact_hersh?currentPage=all

> arms. And next time one of our boats goes to the Straits of Hormuz, start a shoot-up."[7]

Fortunately, thanks to the courage of the head of CENTCOM, Admiral Fallon, who opposed initiating a reckless war with Iran and resigned rather than carry it out, this plan was not put into action during the Bush administration.

The material discussed in this book challenges us to question our assumptions and conditioned responses. Nowhere are these factors more of an issue than when discussing 9/11. The official version of the terrorist attacks was formulated quickly and repeated over and over again; along with looped images of planes crashing into the Twin Towers and the towers collapsing. Any questioning of the official account was met with blithe or angry rejection of what George W. Bush called "outrageous conspiracy theories" that he commanded the corporate media and the American people to "not tolerate."[8] As Americans and the rest of the world learned painfully since 9/11, George W. Bush is not exactly George Washington when it comes to telling the truth (Saddam has weapons of mass destruction, Iraq was involved in 9/11, the fundamentals of our economy are sound, etc.). If the U.S. Government has been caught repeatedly lying and if the corporate media does nothing more than repeat what is told to them by government officials, do we not have good reasons to examine the events of 9/11 for ourselves?

If you are just starting your investigation of 9/11, World Trade Center Seven is a great place to start. WTC 7 was not struck by an airplane and was not, unlike other WTC buildings that remained standing, heavily damaged by the collapse of either of the twin towers. Yet, this 47 story steel skyscraper that was specifically designed to withstand a terror attack or extreme weather conditions collapsed at near freefall speed in a symmetrical fashion into its own footprint at 5:20 p.m. on

7 "Cheney, Neocons Considered Killing Americans in Pretext to Attack Iran" by Kurt Nimmo. http://www.prisonplanet.com/cheney-neocons-considered-killing-americans-in-pretext-to-attack-iran.html

8 "White House Targets Conspiracy Theorists as Terrorist Recruiters" by Paul Joseph Watson. The article contains the video clip of Bush's statement. http://www.prisonplanet.com/articles/september2006/070906terroristrecruiters.htm

the afternoon of September 11, 2001.[9] Witnesses Barry Jennings and Michael Hess, both high level NYC employees, reported experiencing explosions in WTC 7 even before the twin towers had collapsed.[10] The BBC reported that WTC 7, also called the Salomon Brothers building, had collapsed "as the result of this morning's attacks" *before* it had actually collapsed. Incredibly, this report was conducted by reporter Jane Standley with the WTC 7 still visible in the skyline behind her.[11]

The official story explanation is that fire, along with a new phenomenon called "thermal expansion," brought down WTC 7. It took seven years for the government to land on this theory after previous explanations featured in the oft-cited Popular Mechanics article[12] of extensive damage from the collapsing twin towers and the supposed explosion of a fuel oil tank were shown to be false. NIST admits that they did not look for any evidence of explosives and yet their finding that fire brought down WTC 7 is cited as scientific by defenders of the government account.

Real science, not computer model pseudo-science, is beginning to take place in regard to the collapse of all three skyscrapers on 9/11. One of the best organizations as far as conducting and compiling scientific evidence for what happened on 9/11 is Architects and Engineers for 9/11 Truth, which now consists of over 900 architectural and engineering professionals.[13] Members

9 Many videos of this are available. http://www.youtube.com/watch?v=LD06SAf0p9A&feature=related is one of them. *Loose Change: Final Cut* by Dylan Avery and Jason Bermas goes into a detailed analysis of the WTC 7 collapse and surrounding issues. http://video.google.com/videoplay?docid=-3719259008768610598

10 Barry Jennings is now reported dead (but may be in witness protection). Michael Hess changed his story to conform to the official version. See "Michael Hess, WTC 7 explosion witness" http://www.youtube.com/watch?v=BUfiLbXMa64 and "Barry Jennings-9/11 WTC 7 Full Uncut Interview" http://www.youtube.com/watch?v=VQY-ksiuwKU

11 "BBC Reports Collapse of WTC 7 Early-TWICE" http://www.youtube.com/watch?v=6mxFRigYD3s This clip is also featured in *Loose Change: Final Cut*. BBC made this report because of a report on an internal Reuters newswire.

12 "Debunking the 9/11 Myths: Special Report" http://www.popularmechanics.com/technology/military_law/1227842.html?page=5

13 I highly recommend this website, http://www.ae911truth.org/ Especially important is the "Technical Articles" section that includes over 50 articles written by scientists and professionals.

of this organization have published articles in peer-reviewed science journals, including a crucial article called "Active Thermitic Material Discovered in Dust from the 9/11 World Trade Center Catastrophe."[14] This article conclusively shows that explosives were present in the dust from the World Trade Center on September 11, 2001.

The collapses themselves are not the only part of the official 9/11 conspiracy theory to be greatly discredited, however. The airplane hijackings that the official story rests on are quite dubious. There is no hard evidence that any of the 19 "hijackers" actually boarded the planes. The security camera footage of Mohamed Atta and "Abdulaziz Alomari" that was endlessly looped on television was taken in the Portland airport, not in Boston where the two supposedly boarded Flight 11 and crashed it into the north tower. In reality, Alomari could not have been a hijacker because he was still alive and well after 9/11.[15] In fact, six of the alleged hijackers have been reported to be alive and well by news agencies all over the world.[16]

Assuming the hijackers did successfully board the planes with box cutters in tow, there are still serious problems with the official story. None of the four planes sent out a signal that they had been hijacked. This is, of course, something pilots are trained to do if an unauthorized person attempts to enter the cockpit. How could "hijackers" like the diminutive Hani Hanjour (5'4" tall), take over a cockpit from pilots and co-pilots, who in several cases were ex-military and quite large and athletic men, all without the pilots even hitting the hijack alarm? Even assuming they gained control of the cockpit, the technical expertise to fly jets into precise targets is quite an impressive skill. Hani Hanjour, a man whose flight instructors had serious doubts about his ability to fly a Cessna, was supposedly able to navigate what is normally the most heavily protected airspace in the world over an hour after Flight 11 went off course, execute a hairpin 270 degree turn,

14 This article appears in *The Open Chemical Physics Journal*. http://www.bentham-open.org/pages/content.php?TOCPJ/2009/00000002/00000001/7TOCPJ.SGM

15 "Resurrected Hijackers" from 9-11 Research. http://911research.wtc7.net/disinfo/deceptions/identities.html

16 Ibid

and slam Flight 77 into the part of the Pentagon that was under construction and contained mainly civilian employees.[17]

While no hijacking signal or suspicious radio communication from the cockpits was sent out, air traffic controllers were quickly aware something was wrong when the jets went off course, or in some cases disappeared from radar. The standard operating procedure for intercepting aircraft was changed in June 2001 by Dick Cheney.[18] This change made it so that the only Dick Cheney could order fighter jets to pursue the hijacked aircraft.[19] He did not exercise that authority. Instead, he ordered NORAD to stand down.[20] Three months after 9/11, Cheney returned this authority to NORAD.

The other crucial element that has been reported on briefly but largely ignored by the corporate media is the war games executed on 9/11. At least six different war game exercises were conducted on the morning of 9/11, including Operation Northern Vigilance, Operation Vigilant Guardian, and Operation Vigilant Warrior. These war games "coincidentally" involved scenarios involving hijacked planes. "Blips" were inserted into FAA radar as part of the exercise which led one employee, when told of a real hijacking, to ask, "Is this real world or exercise?"[21] Not only did these war games have the effect of confusing air traffic controllers and quite probably military personnel, they also conveniently moved many of the fighter jets that would have been in the area to the north or south. Dick Cheney just happened to have command over these exercises and over the response to the hijackings and is one of the few individuals who knew what was really going on during the false flag attacks of 9/11.[22] The actual mechanism for controlling the attacks is still murky, but it likely involved risk-management software from Ptech as well as a modern incar-

---

17 Ibid (This information is verifiable in a number of different places)

18 "War Games Were Cover for the Operational Execution of 9/11" by Alex Jones and Paul Joseph Watson. http://www.prisonplanet.com/articles/september2004/080904wargamescover.htm

19 See "Twenty Minutes with the President" by Charlie Sheen. http://www.infowars.com/twenty-minutes-with-the-president/

20 Ibid

21 "Wargames Were Cover for the Operational Execution of 9/11" by Alex Jones and Paul Joseph Watson. http://www.prisonplanet.com/articles/september2004/080904wargamescover.htm

22 Ibid

nation of PROMISE software that was able to access all of the necessary computer systems.[23]

Pentagon survivor April Gallop is currently suing the U.S. Government for injuries she and her son sustained when she sat down at her desk on September 11. She asserts that she saw no evidence of a large jet hitting the building and that the damage that was caused to the Pentagon was at least partially the result of explosives going off very close to her work station.[24]

There is a growing awareness of people all over the world that 9/11 was an inside job. There are generally two groups of people that individuals fall into when asked about 9/11. The first group believes the official story but has not researched the issue for themselves. This is either out of ignorance of the issue or an unwillingness to consider "conspiracy theories." The second group consists of those who used to believe the official story, but now have changed their minds because of the incredible amount of evidence that the official account of 9/11 is almost completely fictional.[25]

Realizing that the government, and by extension the corporate media, have lied about 9/11 can be a traumatic experience. Many people find that they also must question other aspects of their belief system. Satan has capitalized on this tendency by having his Luciferian minions put out a lot of disinformation about Christianity and especially about Jesus himself. In the film *Zeitgeist*, for example, Peter Joseph mixes real information about 9/11 and the power of the Federal Reserve with unsupported garbage about the "true origins" of Christianity.[26] According to

---

23 Listen to episode 97 of the Corbett Report, "9/11/09 and the Bigger, Bigger Picture" as well as episode 45, "Ptech and the 9/11 software." http://www.corbettreport.com/index.php?i=Episodes I highly recommend all of the work James Corbett does at www.corbettreport.com

24 Ms. Gallop's lawsuit can be viewed here: http://rawstory.com/news/2008/911_survivor_blasts_Rumsfeld_Cheney_No_1217.html

25 There are hundreds of websites and dozens of films and books on the subject. I recommend the work by Alex Jones (several films), David Ray Griffin (several excellent books), Webster Tarpley's book *9/11 Synthetic Terror*, and Jonathan Ellinoff's excellent film *Core of Corruption*. There is plenty of disinformation out there too, but I am confident that there is plenty of verifiable and solid information to destroy the official story 100 times over.

26 This will be addressed in the next chapter. I highly recommend "Zeitgeist Refuted Final Cut" by Elliot Nesch. http://www.youtube.com/watch?v=GYNmFQkHBaE&feature=channel

*Zeitgeist*, Jesus was nothing more than a version of a common myth about a god born on December 25th, crucified, and resurrected in three days.[27]

The reason this is important is that the biggest false flag attack is currently being planned and perpetrated, and the patsy is Christianity. Religion in general, but especially Christianity, is being attacked as the cause of war and the main tool of control used by the elite. Unfortunately, there is a modicum of truth in this accusation if we look at the institutional religious political systems that pose as Christianity. If we look closer, however, we see that the Crusades and other oft-cited examples have nothing to do with Christ and everything to do with the ceaseless struggle for political power. The sound bite that "religion causes wars" is uncritically accepted by large numbers of people both in America and around the world.[28] This is a crucial talking point for Satan's minions as they ready the world for Lucifer's great deception.

Albert Pike, the Satan-worshipping leader of Scottish Rite Freemasonry and author of *Morals and Dogma*, made the prediction that there would be three world wars. The first would overthrow the Russian Tsars and set up a stronghold for atheistic communism. The second would be fought between Political Zionists and fascists and would result in the establishment of a Jewish state in Palestine. The third world war that this Luciferian agent predicted will pit Political Zionists and their supporters against the followers and nations of Islam. Pike believed that through this method the three major Monotheistic religions—Judaism, Islam, and Christianity, would be all but decimated and the world would be ready to abandon them. With the monotheistic religions crippled, Pike believed the way would be clear for Luciferian doctrine to finally be taught openly.

> We shall unleash the Nihilists and Atheists, and we shall provoke a formidable social cataclysm which in all its horror will show clearly to the nations the effect of absolute atheism, origin of savagery and of the most bloody turmoil. Then everywhere, the citizens, obliged to defend themselves against the world minority of revolutionaries, will exterminate those destroyers of civilization, and the multi-

27 Ibid

28 "Religious Wars, Fact or Fiction" by Chris White (nowheretorun1984). http://www.youtube.com/watch?v=eO3E-Q6lQfQ

> tude, disillusioned with christianity [sic], whose deistic spirits will be from that moment without compass (direction), anxious for an ideal, but without knowing where to render its adoration, will receive the true light through the universal manifestation of the pure doctrine of Lucifer brought finally out in the public view, a manifestation which will result from the general reactionary movement which will follow the destruction of christianity [sic] and atheism, both conquered and exterminated at the same time.[29]

We can already see the machinations and preparations for World War III as well as the obvious intention of Satan and his minions to not only initiate this conflict but to blame it on believers in God. The doctrine of Lucifer, as Pike calls it, will be the basis for a one world religion. Luciferian doctrine currently permeates our media, our schools, and our social sciences. But, it is not yet overt. These teachings and satanic principles are being brought more and more out into the open, oftentimes by the "alternative" voices who claim to be fighting against the New World Order. We will examine these false teachers in the next chapter.

29 Quote from Albert Pike taken from William Guy Carr's book, *Pawns in the Game* (1958). http://yamaguchy.netfirms.com/7897401/carr/pawns_index.html

# Chapter 12

# The Lies of the Truth Movement

> "You think they're selling you truth. The truth is they're selling you out."[1]

For many people, myself included, the realization that mainstream "reality" is in fact a media fabricated mirage is both exhilarating and disorienting. After all, if 9/11 really was an inside job, what else are we being lied to about? This "awakening" leads to some carefully prepared and very dangerous places. Many of the alternative sources of information that readily admit 9/11 was an inside job are also quick to challenge other beliefs that people have. Most notably, however, there is a concerted, and I believe spiritually-coordinated attack on orthodox beliefs about Jesus Christ. The gurus of the Truth Movement include David Icke, Acharya S, Jordan Maxwell, Peter Joseph, and Michael Tsarion. All of them have their own pet teachings about the nature of reality. But, their common thread is denial of Jesus Christ; not just as Savior and Lord, but even as a historical figure.

The technique that these "researchers" use is to mix real information about the truly insidious nature of the New World Order system with false identification of the root of the problems and false solutions. These solutions actually pave the way for the satanic New World Order agenda to go forward. They consistently identify Christianity as a "tool of control" of the establishment elite. They also put forward the idea that Jesus was merely a mythical product

1 From Thrice's song "Hoods on Peregrine" –Check out all of Thrice's excellent and insightful music. www.thrice.net

of ancient occult religions and that there are really many ancient myths about saviors quite similar to the story found in the New Testament gospels. While they deny Jesus with varying degrees of antimony, they all agree that of course Jesus Christ can't save us—we must look to ourselves to find salvation. The doctrine of self-glorification is at the heart of Lucifer's deception. Here is a sampling of what is being taught to truth seekers all over the world.

David Icke, a former soccer player and broadcaster on mainstream British television, is a well spoken and quite good natured individual. His "awakening" occurred partially as a result of hearing voices, partially because of a spiritual experience in the midst of a circle of stones in Peru, and partially from some good old fashioned research. Icke has woken up many people to the New World Order and has been an outspoken critic of government's ever-increasingly totalitarian bent in the Western World. His book[2] contains a lot of very accurate information about the system that does in fact surround us and seeks to manipulate our lives. However, Icke spends the first few pages of his 600+ page book attacking the Biblical view of who we as people are and our place in the universe. Icke claims that we are "Infinite Consciousness" and wants us to realize we are not individuals but instead that we are "the self-aware ALL."[3] Icke claims to be against all religions but he attacks Judeo-Christian beliefs specifically. "There is no beginning and no end, no Alpha and Omega, because all is One."[4] While a Christian will of course find this statement blasphemous, it would seem quite palatable to polytheistic Hindu or a New Ager. Icke goes on to say the following.

> We identify with division and 'parts', not unity. This has happened because of the massive manipulation of our sense of reality that has led us to identify the 'I' with the biological computer we call the body. Look at how many religions claim it is blasphemous to say that you are the All, or what they call 'God'. We can't say we are 'God'; we must be humble and accept that we are subordinate sin-

2 *The David Icke Guide to the Global Conspiracy (and how to end it)* – Icke has written a number of books, but this one covers his major arguments and it's the only one I have read.

3 *The David Icke Guide to the Global Conspiracy (and how to end it)* (pp. 2-3)

4 Ibid p. 3

> ners who must cower in the face of the Almighty. … This nonsense is designed by those who control the religions (not the programmed underlings in the funny hats) to lock us into the computer level of perception, the level at which we are easy to shepherd and pen. Listen to the language of religion- 'The Lord is your shepherd and you are part of the flock.'[5]
>
> What pain and suffering has been caused by the religions which talk of judgment days and some 'God' choosing who does and who does not have eternal life. They tell us that only if we believe in the non-existent 'Jesus' can we qualify for eternity.[6]

This claim that Jesus did not really exist is hard to justify on any objective historical basis. However, it is readily proclaimed by many of the Truth Movement's gurus. Icke goes on later in the book to make the thoroughly debunked but oft-repeated claim that Jesus is synonymous with the mythical god Horus.[7]

When analyzing the above claims from David Icke, it is important to remember that they are contained in a book that contains a lot of great information that anyone just awakening from the fake mainstream "reality" may find compelling. Once again, when our "reality" is shattered, there really is an opportunity for Satan to come in and seed lies about Jesus. If we believe lies about Jesus Christ, whom Satan and his minions fear above all else, then he does not really care what we do know the truth about. Icke is far from the only person spreading this particular lie.

D.M. Murdock, better known by her former pen name of Acharya S, is a big proponent of the idea that Jesus was nothing more than a recycled version of the Egyptian god Horus. Unlike some gurus, Acharya does at least try to include some historical support for her claims. In fact, it is accurate to say that sun worship has been very popular, not only in Egypt, but throughout ancient and even not so ancient civilizations. It is also accurate that much of the symbolism and iconography of the Catholic Church has been defiled with the influence of sun and fertility cults. Furthermore, the dates of some "Christian" holidays such

5 Ibid p. 3

6 Ibid p. 3

7 Ibid p. 126 An excellent resource for researching these claims is Greg Boyd's *Jesus: Lord or Legend? wrestling with the Jesus dilemma* or Elliot Nesch's short film *Zeitgeist Refuted Final Cut.*

as Christmas and Easter coincide with important dates of "astro-theology," as well as sun and fertility cults. It is clear that the sun worshipping cults that were still quite strong in the Roman Empire took an "if you can't beat them, join them" approach to Christianity from the reign of Constantine forward. This resulted in the often blasphemous and non-orthodox Catholic Church. It is a spurious argument, however, to claim that this corrupt hybridization of the Catholic Church refutes Christianity and somehow proves that Jesus Christ was a new version of the Horus myth. However, this is precisely what Acharya would have us believe.

> There remains much more about the solar origins of Christianity and the solar nature of Jesus Christ beginning from the earliest times to the latest. Suffice it to say that this equation did not begin or end in the 19th century with any particular group or individual but, rather, has a long history within Christian tradition itself, as we can see proved abundantly here and elsewhere, such as in my books.
>
> In the end, we need to ask ourselves: Is it more scientifically plausible that 2,000 years ago *the* God of the cosmos took birth through the womb of a virgin as a Jewish man who walked on water, performed miracles, raised the dead, resurrected himself from death and ascended into heaven – or could it be that this tale is a reworking of older myths in currency around the known world of the time?[8]

Isn't it interesting that Acharya encourages us to "ask ourselves" if the Biblical account of Jesus is really "scientifically plausible?" Satan's continual lie, from the Garden of Eden forward, is that we do not need God to guide us. That we can figure out what is right, wrong, and true for ourselves. This lie is mixed in with the magic word of the modern age, "science," which is of course presented as anathema to Christianity.

Jordan Maxwell (not his real name), is one of the most powerful and longest tenured gurus in the Truth Movement. His website[9] contains a mix of some quality information and links, lots and lots of hating on Christianity, and somewhat random links to Google searches that Maxwell claims are quite important. The basic claim that Maxwell makes is that Christianity and the

8 Excerpt from *Jesus Christ as the Sun God Throughout History* by Acharya S.
9 www.jordanmaxwell.com

church is a tool of control used by the elite. Here is his response to the question of whether or not he believes in God.

> Yes, most certainly! Jordan has always believed in the presence of God. But he is also well-aware, through years of study, that man-made religions are the product of "The Powers That Be." Jordan sees no problem whatsoever with the words and teachings attributed to Jesus in the Bible's New Testament.
>
> Jordan believes that the Bible — both Old and New Testaments — is a profoundly important work of benefit to mankind. This is especially true of the New Testament story of Jesus. Jordan believes that the New Testament is a brilliantly conceived story which is in fact an *encoded metaphor*. The correct understanding of the metaphor in the New Testament story have [sic] been purposely concealed by the Church throughout the ages.
>
> In Jordan's view, the entire belief system we call Christianity, in all of its various forms and denominations (not the Bible) as it exists in the world today, is a fraud foisted on the unsuspecting peoples of the world. Overall, the Church is a world-wide money-grubbing criminal conspiracy, owned behind the scenes by "The Powers That Be." In Jordan's view, it is time for the Christian Establishment world-wide to be seen for what it really is: **an enemy of both God and factual Truth.**
>
> Jordan further feels that the entire Christian church in the world today is a creation of the same "Powers That Be" who have given us the corrupt world that we live in. It is time for the Christian Church to be exposed for the profound evil that it represents in this world. It is also time for the encoded metaphor, hidden for years, to be brought to light for the benefit of those who recognize that there is nothing of any redeemable value in the Christian church today, and who wish to worship God "in Spirit and in Truth." In the very near future, Jordan will be presenting the encoded metaphor for the first time here on his website.
>
> In conclusion, Jordan has the highest of respect for the Divine Presence in the universe that men have called "God," and believes that the New Testament is a profound and brilliantly-written metaphor which needs to be explained to those who are sincerely longing and searching for the truth of our existence. Explaining for the first time the encoded metaphor in the New Testament is surely now "an idea whose time has come." This hidden encoded story will be presented by Jordan Maxwell on this website very soon.[10]

10 Ibid

In other words, reading the Bible in a straightforward manner will surely cause us to be deceived and trapped by the powers that be. But, if we look to Maxwell for answers, he will reveal the meaning of the "encrypted metaphor." Maxwell's message, which just happens to dovetail well with the New Age teachings of today, is that while there is a "Divine Presence," the Bible's accounts and descriptions of God are not accurate. If you watch Maxwell's presentations, it soon becomes obvious that his teachings are based on interpreting everything as symbolic. And, through a strange method of "interpreting" the "real" meanings of words with no apparent consideration of the fact that the Bible was written in languages other than English.[11]

Much of Maxwell's work is a rehashing of Manley P. Hall and Helena Blavatsky's work (both Luciferians). Maxwell's emphasis on symbols and redefining words in the name of exposing the New World Order is actually "externalizing the hierarchy," to paraphrase the title of Alice Bailey's book.[12] In other words, the occult teachings of the secret societies are being broadcast to a much wider audience. This is an effort to get more people to delve into the spiritual world from a perspective that is not only non-Christian; but one that approaches Christianity as an enemy. More importantly, it is enticing people to accept that Jesus Christ is just a myth, metaphor, or just one of several examples of Christ consciousness.

Peter Joseph (not his full name), is the producer of the movies *Zeitgeist* and *Zeitgeist: Addendum*. The original *Zeitgeist* follows a similar pattern to Icke's book discussed above. Joseph begins by presenting the "Jesus myth" theory-which he takes mainly from the work of Jordan Maxwell and Acharya S.[13] Joseph then goes on in the next two parts of the film to offer real information about the Federal Reserve monetary system and false flag

11 See Chris White's (nowheretorun1984) videos "William Cooper debunks Jordan Maxwell" http://www.youtube.com/watch?v=zD1Vf5hoRfQ&feature=PlayList&p=2A4A414FECF6AE30&index=0 and "Debunking Jordan Maxwell" http://www.youtube.com/watch?v=jwugLx2rSJY&feature=fvw

12 Bailey wrote *Externalization of the Hierarchy* (which of course advocated the perfectibility of man) under the possession of spirit she called the "Tibetan."

13 Check out www.zeitgeistchallenge.com for the offer of a cash prize for anyone who can provide primary source evidence for the claims of *Zeitgeist* part one.

terrorism. The good information was mainly taken from Alex Jones's films without prior permission. Like much of the material in the Truth Movement, *Zeitgeist* combines real information about the corrupt system of political and economic power with straw man and completely fraudulent attacks on Christianity. For example, Joseph attempts to make a big deal out of the fact that Horus was born on December 25$^{th}$. Anyone who has studied the Bible or church history knows Jesus was born either in the spring or the fall, but not in December. This date was chosen by the paganized Catholic Church in approximately A.D. 354 and is of no real importance to historical Christianity.

*Zeitgeist: Addendum* is even more clearly satanic New World Order propaganda while posing as the opposite. While continuing to bash the existing order, Joseph proposes a solution called the "resource based economy" which is possible only through completely centralizing power and ensuring that everyone goes along with the system. Joseph suggests basing this system on the load of the earth and wants us to develop a "modern, non-superstitious based understanding of what we are and how we align with nature, to which we are a part."[14] This "understanding" certainly seems to align with the eugenics agenda disguised as environmentalism that is being used to set up the New World Order system of centralized control. Obviously, the system Joseph suggests strongly resembles the scientific dictatorship envisioned by the New World Order, despite the fact the film is supposedly anti-establishment. Joseph, in an interview/debate with Alex Jones, argued that there is no good and evil, no us against them, and that all the problems in the world are the result of improper environmental conditioning and the system of using money.[15] The idea that man does not have a sin nature and that we can create our own utopia is of course one of Satan's oldest lies.

Peter Joseph is also the originator of the Zeitgeist Movement. Here is the mission statement.

> The Zeitgeist Movement is a grass roots campaign to unify the world through a common ideology based on the fundamentals of life and nature. This movement ignores politics, religion and the

14 www.zeitgeistmovie.com/statement.htm

15 See "Alex Jones – Peter Joseph" http://www.youtube.com/watch?v=_oTDXXh463g

> like, and instead attempts to communicate how all humans are the same at the fundamental level and how it is time we start to work together on a global scale to end the seemingly perpetual conflict and suffering in our current world society.[16]

How convenient for the world elite that those "waking up" to reality and the New World Order are being funneled into the belief that we need to "work together on a global scale" through a "common ideology" which of course ignores that silly old thing called religion and the imaginary character of Jesus Christ. In order to get people to adopt belief in a one world Lucifer-worshipping religion, Satan must first break down people's faith in traditional religions. In this particular area of propaganda it is crucial for Satan's minions to associate Jesus with religious institutions and to associate religions with the political establishment. It is only after people reject the old paradigms, whether fraudulent or not, that they can be enticed to embrace overt Luciferian doctrine.

Michael Tsarion is one of the most vehement and vocal haters of not just Christianity and Judaism but of Christians and Jews. His particular shtick is that he is an "alternative historian" who claims that humans are the products of alien genetic experimentation. He, like the Freemasons, the Rosicrucians (of which he is a member), and other occult groups, is fascinated with the concept of Atlantis[17] as well as something he calls the "Irish origin of civilization." He teaches that the God of the Bible is really an evil, vengeful, woman-hating terror. Tsarion also espouses the belief that the good god (Lucifer), will send some nice aliens to help us have a wonderful elevation of consciousness in 2012.[18] It will be wonderful for all the enlightened ones that is, but those of us backward knaves who cling to our outdated religion may have to be forcefully eliminated, so that we do not hold everyone else back.

16 www.zeitgeistmovie.com/statement.htm

17 Chris Pinto has done a great job of explaining how occultists view America as the "New Atlantis" and how this ideology has had an influence on America's development in his lecture "The Atlantis Connection" available here http://www.radioliberty.com/vatlantis.html . Chris White also did a podcast featuring this material and a YouTube version called "The Atlantis Connection – Chris Pinto" available here http://www.youtube.com/view_play_list?p=6CB8AB97C7451B56

18 See "2012 Debunked" by Chris White (nowheretorun1984). http://www.youtube.com/watch?v=AUnINDZolDY

Tsarion relies on several of the tricks that Maxwell employs; including playing word games to convince people that the Bible is a secret symbolic code and that the people and places (such as Jesus and Nazareth) did not really exist. Here is a sample of his deceptive tactics, along with the transcript of his trip to the intellectual woodshed courtesy of Chris White's "Tsarion is Wrong: a Debunkumentary." Tsarion's words are italicized.

> *We've all heard of Jesus of Nazareth of course...Jesus from Nazareth. The only trouble is; there is no such place as Nazareth. There never has been a place called Nazareth. The word in fact derives from the Egyptian word "nazir," meaning prince who is sent and also from "nasir" meaning Sirius. The star Sirius. So it is really Jesus of na-Sirius. Furthermore, the word "carpenter," and Jesus was a carpenter remember...Well the word carpenter comes from the semetic nagar, which means serpent priests.* (Quoted from *Origins and Oracles*) [White's response] There are lots of problems here. First, on the assertion that Nazareth never existed: I've heard people say that Nazareth was invented in the fourth century, but I've never understood how one could believe it, because, whether you trust them or not, the Biblical texts date back to the early part of the first century. Even the skeptical scholars do not try to push the gospels much past one hundred A.D. So you have the accounts of this small town of Nazareth in those texts, not to mention the Talmud, which is also in the first century and which obviously does not support the idea of Jesus being the Messiah at all and would have no reason to validate this story. In fact, [the Talmud writers] were clearly looking for holes in the story. But, they mention Jesus in the context of trying to explain away his miracles as parlor tricks. So the question is, why didn't anyone just say the gospels had made up a town called Nazareth? There was a window of a few hundred years where skeptics of the day had a chance to say "these gospel writers have gone and made up a town" and they would've been in a much better position to know if the town had existed or not because they were locals. On this point it seems that Tsarion is simply using the stated fact that Nazareth was little more than an outpost of a town, and using it as proof that it didn't exist.
>
> Let's move on. Nazir and nasir have different consonants. He gives no reason to jump from one to the other, but it's obvious he needs to get there somehow to make it sound like Sirius. Not to mention the fact that Sirius does not mean serpent. Sirius comes from the Greek seirios which means scorcher. The rise of Sirius happens in the season of greatest heat, summer. It's close to spelling

> streblos which means "twisted," but again, they are two different words and neither of them matches up with Tsarion's definition. The word for carpenter in the New Testament is Tekton. In Aramaic it's nagger, which can mean craftsman or possibly even scholar, but there is no good support for Tsarion's claim that the Aramaic word nagger means serpent priests. Again, this shows that he has a specific target in these deceptions.[19]

Believe it or not, this is not a rare error in Tsarion's scholarship as presented in *Origins and Oracles*; you may want to save your 320 dollars for something else. White was able to debunk many of Tsarion's claims fairly easily. But, unfortunately, many people accept them at face value without critically examining them. Once people have their mainstream reality shattered they are susceptible to alternative theories about many things. This is especially alluring if those theories get rid of those unpleasant Christian teachings about sin and hell, and about the need for Jesus Christ to be our only Savior, Redeemer, and Lord. All of the false teachers in the Truth Movement appeal to man's desire to feel special and smart. Most importantly, the false teachers also tap into the Luciferian lie that man can attain higher levels, and ultimately godhood, through themselves.

Unfortunately, it is not just the Truth Movement that is propagating Luciferian doctrine. The corporate media, entertainment, and movie industries work for the leaders of the New World Order and ultimately for the leader of the New World Order, Satan himself. We will explore the enemy's brainwashing campaign in the next chapter.

19 Transcribed from "Michael Tsarion is Wrong: A Debunkumentary" by Frank Lorde and Chris White with minor edits by the writer.

# Chapter 13

# The Media Matrix

"Unfortunately, no one can be told what the matrix is. You have to see it for yourself."[1]

One of the most common characteristics of people who "wake up" to the satanic New World Order system is the inability to take television seriously. Once the illusion of the media matrix is broken, I have found in my own experience that I cannot watch television talking heads, or "entertainment" programming, without noticing lie after lie and feeling that I am watching nothing but propaganda. This propaganda is specifically designed to lead me away from God. Hopefully, investigating the claims that I put forward in this book will help you see the media matrix for the pseudo-reality that it is. Unfortunately, there is no special process I can recommend, other than to start getting your information from sources other than the corporate media. If you feel you must watch television, try and watch with skeptical and discerning eyes.

There has been a great deal of writing in Christian circles that quite correctly decries the sexual, violent, and anti-family content of our media-saturated culture. Sexual immorality is glorified incessantly, gratuitous violence is pervasive, and trying to find a well-functioning family with father, mother, and children behaving in Biblically obedient ways is like looking for a teetotaler on Bourbon Street during Mardi Gras. However, there is usually something missing from critiques of American media. It

1 A quote from the character Morpheus in the film *The Matrix* http://en.wikiquote.org/wiki/The_Matrix

is the understanding that these outrages are deliberately planned and executed in order to break down the institutions that are the biggest threat to the power monopoly of New World Order corporate state: the church, the family, and the individual. My critique will focus on informational and educational media because the messages in entertainment programming parrot the messages of the news media. People may be less likely, however, to identify the news media as carefully scripted, controlled, and manipulated for specific ends.

The first myth, or illusion, that must be shattered is that the media in America is free and independent to act as a "watchdog" on government and large corporations. In reality, the media is controlled by the same small group of elites that control government. While the plethora of cable news channels, local television stations, and newspapers gives the illusion of a broad range of discourse, the reality is that five mega corporations control between 80-90% of the world's media outlets.[2] Media control in America is certainly not new, although recent consolidation has certainly made things worse. J.P. Morgan found that it was only necessary to control the top 25 newspapers to control the general publishing policy of the rest of the nation's newspapers. He set up the Council on Foreign Relations specifically to control the press.[3] Much of the control of the behind the scenes controllers can be seen in what is and what is not considered newsworthy. As media critic Michael Parenti states, "The media may not always be able to tell us what to think, but they are strikingly successful in telling us what to think about."[4]

Any doubt that what is discussed in the media is controlled can be dispelled by watching the newscasts for the major networks or the cable news channels on the same day. The same four to five stories will be the "top stories" on every channel. Watch the commercials; the same drug-company ads will be everywhere—sometimes even in the same order. Perhaps an argument could be

2 These corporations are General Electric, Walt Disney, News Corp., Time Warner, and Viacom. http://www.freepress.net/ownership/chart/main

3 See "The CFR Controls American News/Media" which sources the congressional record from 1917. http://vodpod.com/watch/554980-the-cfr-controls-american-newsmedia

4 As quoted in *Rule by Secrecy* by Jim Marrs (102).

made that these stories truly are the most important, and that explains their presence on every channel. This is quickly dispelled, however, when "top stories" include celebrity gossip or scandal.

The corporate media and its controllers love salacious stories about scandals in the personal lives of politicians and other celebrities for several reasons. First, these stories provide a distraction. If people are focused on Michael Jackson's death for weeks, then they aren't focused on bills making their way through congress that will cripple the economy, or the fact that select banks have received 23.7 trillion dollars in loans, guarantees, and bailouts.[5]

Second, these stories provide the illusion of an uncontrolled press because of attacks on supposedly very powerful people. For example, the entire world found out about Bill Clinton's marital infidelity and heard his lies after the fact. What people didn't hear about, however, was the fact that Clinton was selling nuclear weapons technology to China.[6] The savage media frenzy around relatively small issues propagates the illusion that if there was a really big scandal (like 9/11 being an inside job); the media would be right on top of it and ready to expose it.

Third, the scandal stories provide a way to blackmail politicians and to burn those individuals who show any semblance of resistance to the big banks. It is no accident that governors Elliot Spitzer, Rod Blagojevich, Mark Sanford, and Senator Richard Durbin were all savagely attacked in the media for various scandals and indiscretions shortly after standing up against the Federal Reserve member banks in various ways.[7] Power corrupts, and because they are easy to blackmail and manipulate, the elites prefer to put the corrupt in positions of power. It is also important to realize that the destruction of a particular politician's career does nothing to damage the New World Order system as a whole. Another puppet is simply inserted and the machine keeps right on robbing the people and taking away their freedom.

5 "U.S. Bailouts Could Cost 23.7 Trillion, Inspector General Says" by Thomas R. Eddlem of the New American. http://www.thenewamerican.com/index.php/usnews/election/1475

6 "Scientist: Clinton Administration Gave China Top Nuclear Secrets" by Christopher Ruddy of Newsmax. http://archive.newsmax.com/articles/?a=1999/3/11/55955

7 "Governors Discover Resisting the Fed Has Consequences" by Kevin Jones. http://www.infowars.com/governors-discover-resisting-the-fed-has-consequences/

While the controllers of the media are often able to keep important stories that would be harmful to the establishment out of the press by focusing on red herrings, there are times when a story is too big to ignore and when a big lie must be told and sold to the public. The concept of the "big lie" was extolled by Hitler in Mein Kampf.

> All this was inspired by the principle–which is quite true in itself–that in the big lie there is always a certain force of credibility; because the broad masses of a nation are always more easily corrupted in the deeper strata of their emotional nature than consciously or voluntarily; and thus in the primitive simplicity of their minds they more readily fall victims to the big lie than the small lie, since they themselves often tell small lies in little matters but would be ashamed to resort to large-scale falsehoods. It would never come into their heads to fabricate colossal untruths, and they would not believe that others could have the impudence to distort the truth so infamously. Even though the facts which prove this to be so may be brought clearly to their minds, they will still doubt and waver and will continue to think that there may be some other explanation. For the grossly impudent lie always leaves traces behind it, even after it has been nailed down, a fact which is known to all expert liars in this world and to all who conspire together in the art of lying.[8]

It is not enough to invent a big lie and tell it once, however. The lie must be repeated over and over again to be effective. Joseph Goebbels, a man who knew a thing or two about effective propaganda, had this to say about the big lie:

> The essential English leadership secret does not depend on particular intelligence. Rather, it depends on a remarkably stupid thickheadedness. The English follow the principle that when one lies, one should lie big, and stick to it. They keep up their lies, even at the risk of looking ridiculous.[9]

---

8 Quote taken from the excellent article "Scientists Confirm the Effectiveness of The Big Lie—People Will Go to Extraordinary Lengths to Create False Justifications for Government Misdeeds" by the blogger known as George Washington. http://www.prisonplanet.com/scientists-confirm-the-effectiveness-of-the-big-lie-people-will-go-to-extraordinary-lengths-to-create-false-justifications-for-government-misdeeds.html

9 Ibid

Unfortunately, it is not just the Germans and the British who have had powerful empires supported by a foundation of big lies. The current state of Empire America can be traced back to justification based on 9/11. The official account of 9/11 may well be the biggest of the big lies told in modern times.

The New World Order media controllers laid the foundation for the official narrative months before 9/11. Osama bin Laden was little known to most Americans until the summer of 2001, even though he was already a well-known terrorist and had been wanted by the FBI for years. During the summer months of 2001, however, there were enough stories about bin Laden and terrorism that when 9/11 came around, people were primed and ready to blame bin Laden.[10] Chris White calls this the "Bubba Effect," after a local radio personality who reported on the air that he "just had a feeling" that bin Laden was the one responsible for 9/11.[11]

On the day of 9/11, this "feeling" that people had was carefully nurtured by "inside information" from government sources that all just happened to point at Osama bin Laden and Al Qaeda as being the only terrorist group of pulling off such a brazen and large scale attack. As Jason Bermas points out in his excellent documentary *Fabled Enemies*, "within hours of the attacks on the trade center there seemed to be one suspect, billionaire terrorist Osama bin Laden."[12] Without investigation or inquiry, the corporate media told the American people exactly who to blame. Easy answers and cartoonishly simple enemies are crucial to effective propaganda.

Advertisers and television producers know that images connect more powerfully with the human brain than logical arguments. In the aftermath of 9/11, viewers of any newscast were subjected to the image of a plane hitting the towers and the tow-

---

10 Both Bill Cooper and Alex Jones predicted 9/11. Cooper's prediction was based specifically on a CNN interview with bin Laden. See "Bill Cooper predicts 9-11" http://www.youtube.com/watch?v=EPcia9hQohY&feature=PlayList&p=590FA637164BA752&playnext=1&playnext_from=PL&index=15

11 Chris has mentioned this several times on the Frank and Chris Show. http://frankandchrisshow.com/

12 *Fabled Enemies* is available for order from infowars.com. It can also be viewed free in its entirety on YouTube. http://www.youtube.com/watch?v=28tE0fKpISM&feature=fvst

ers collapsing. These images were played over and over again so that in people's subconscious minds the plane hitting the building was equated with the building collapsing. While physics and peer reviewed scientific journal articles[13] show convincingly that the planes were not responsible for the total collapse of WTC 1 and 2 (much less WTC 7), people are often unable to even consider the possibility that something other than hijacked aircraft brought the towers down. This is because of the effectiveness of the images replayed over and over again.

The key to the effectiveness of the corporate media's sale of the official story and ongoing agenda is not logic and evidence. Instead the key is repetition, appeal to base emotions (fear, hatred), and total elimination of contradictory accounts. Emotionally charged words are tied together in ways designed by psychological warfare experts to create beliefs about connections that do not really exist. For example, after 9/11, George W. Bush, Dick Cheney, Condoleezza Rice, and Donald Rumsfeld mentioned 9/11 countless times in close proximity to Iraq and Saddam Hussein. This was usually accompanied by fear inspiring, dumbed-down sound bites like, "We don't want the smoking gun to be a mushroom cloud."[14] Anyone who questioned the official story, or who even questioned the need to attack Iraq, so the implication went, was exposing the country to possible nuclear attack. 9/11 has been used as the ideological foundation for both foreign policy and domestic policy. Therefore, it is necessary for the establishment to maintain the official story of 9/11 in order to provide plausible reasons for its programs. Sociological studies[15] have shown that once people buy into a government claim (i.e. the need to invade Iraq), they tend to ignore contrary evidence

13 The Scholars for 9/11 Truth website has several papers fitting this description. www.911scholars.org The site with the largest compilation of scientific evidence is Architects and Engineers for 9/11 Truth. www.ae911truth.org

14 See countless videos such as "George: Saddam Hussein Has Weapons of Mass Destruction" http://www.youtube.com/watch?v=gMStCHtUNeY&feature=related or "Bush Iraq 9/11 Lies" http://www.youtube.com/watch?v=jTpZYH2x9-k

15 *"There Must Be a Reason": Osama, Saddam, and Inferred Justification* explores the reasons that people clung to the belief that Saddam Hussein was responsible for 9/11 when even the Bush administration admitted he was not. http://sociology.buffalo.edu/documents/hoffmansocinquiryarticle_000.pdf

and "infer justification" for the government's claim, even if that justification is irrational. That explains why people have been so slow to question the official story on 9/11 and so ready to cling to any support for the official story—no matter how illogical and unscientific it is. The media controllers know this psychological tendency. But they also know that it works best when alternative explanations and viewpoints are not ever really considered.

There are many methods that the media controllers use to manipulate public opinion. Some of the most important are the establishment of a paradigmatic parameter of acceptable opinion, repetition of specific talking points that can be mindlessly repeated by the viewer, and vicious personal attacks on anyone who dare speak outside the box.

The most common paradigm that is energized and largely created by the corporate media is the political system of "left" vs. "right." The acceptable parameters of this paradigm are set by establishment gatekeepers. The gatekeepers include, for example, Noam Chomsky and Michael Moore on the left, and Rush Limbaugh and Glenn Beck on the right. Anything outside the bounds of these New World Order media gatekeepers is labeled as conspiracy theory and summarily dismissed.[16] The vast majority of media talking heads fall somewhere in the middle of this false dichotomy. When the Republicans are in power, the Democrats and the left-leaning media claim to be anti-war and pro-civil liberties. When the Democrats gain power, however, the wars continue without protest from the supposedly liberal media. And, civil liberties and individual freedoms continue to be seized under the rhetoric of political correctness as well as the bi-partisan promise of security from dangerous extremists. When the Democrats are in power, Republicans claim they want lower

16 Chomsky and Moore have both flirted with 9/11 truth but Chomsky later claimed there wasn't enough evidence http://georgewashington.blogspot.com/2006/05/chomsky-gets-f.html and Michael Moore included only the weakest, most personal evidence of inside job in Fahrenheit 9/11 and later said that presenting the real evidence would be "un-American." See "Alex Jones-Michael Moore is a Fraud" http://www.youtube.com/watch?v=Yy2QYoT4LWw. Rush Limbaugh will play kook music and dismiss the issue out of hand and Glenn Beck claims that there are no FEMA camps and has called for 9/11 Truthers to be arrested. The reason Chomsky and Moore were more sympathetic was that 9/11 occurred under the "right-wing" Bush administration.

taxes, fiscal responsibility, smaller government, and the protection of free speech and the right to bear arms. When the Republicans regain power, however, the Federal Government continues to expand, taxes increase except for the ultra-rich, expensive foreign wars are defended as necessary—with protest labeled aiding the enemy—and the threat of "terrorists" is used to strip away privacy and personal liberty.

The New World Order agenda continues to move forward regardless of which side of the false paradigm is in power. Government control expands under a number of guises and consequently personal freedom and the ability of individuals, towns, cities, counties, states, and even America to be independent and self-sufficient goes away. This is all carried out in the quest for world government and the ultimate scientific dictatorship. The two-party system, the left-right paradigm, is crucial because it allows the New World Order to offer the illusion of choice while simultaneously maintaining control.[17]

The ceaseless repetition of talking points, sound bites, and easy answers is essential to the effectiveness of corporate media propaganda. The idea is to give people pre-packaged opinions that they can say when talking about the issue with their friends. They are left feeling informed and even occasionally passionate about an issue without remotely understanding it. Some of the common statements regarding 9/11 are, "I do not go in for conspiracy theories," "somebody would blow the whistle on something that big," "the government can't keep secrets," "the government wouldn't kill American citizens," "the terrorists hate us for our freedoms," and many others. Each of these statements is easily refutable, but that does not matter. They appeal to people's laziness, to people's apathy, to people's desire for everything to be okay, and most importantly, to people's pride. People hate to admit they are wrong or that they have been duped, and these sound bites allow them to laugh off and dismiss anything that the corporate media has not given its express approval to consider.

When the corporate media is unable to fully ignore someone who is questioning the official story on 9/11 or any other issue of

17 The best explanation of the false left-right paradigm is given by the man who coined the term, Alex Jones. "The False Left Right System-From the Obama Deception" http://www.youtube.com/watch?v=bF6Dt7SS_yw

importance to the New World Order, the most common approach is to attack him/her using a combination of two logical fallacies: ad hominem argument and circular reasoning. For example, when Willie Nelson questioned the official story because the collapse of the towers looked like controlled demolition to him, Bill O'Reilly attacked him as a "pinhead" and a "conspiracy nut."[18] O'Reilly's name-calling is not backed up by any argument that addresses Willie Nelson's claims. Ironically, Willie Nelson's questioning of the official conspiracy theory inspires O'Reilly, who of course ostensibly believes the government's official conspiracy theory, to call him a "conspiracy nut." Not believing conspiracy theories put forth by the government equals being a conspiracy nut according to O'Reilly's logic.

The message from the media about 9/11 is that questioning the official story is crazy because crazy people are the ones who question 9/11. But, the only reason they are identified as crazy is because they question the official story on 9/11. Around and around we go. The circular reasoning and ad hominem attacks are occasionally backed up by a straw man argument where the media will pick out one conspiracy theory or one element that really is easily refuted (i.e. CGI fakery from the "no planes" disinformation crowd), and pretend that by debunking that that all the questions are answered and the official story is proven correct. Usually, however, the media does not even go this far—preferring instead to ignore the issue and occasionally attack someone who is too prominent to ignore.

All media, including the evening news, is essentially advertising. The supposedly informational media is designed to get people to buy into the agenda of the establishment. The agenda is usually some variation on the supposed necessity of offensive wars in distant lands and the supposed necessity of bailing out massive banks with taxpayer money in order to "save" the economy.

Even more important than the political, social, and economic agendas propagated by the media is the spiritual agenda. The focus is always on the material world. The idea is to fill up the mind with obsessive desires for things that do not matter. Satan knows that we know in our hearts that all is not right in the world. His

18 See "O'Reilly Calls Willie Nelson a Pinhead Over 9/11 Remarks" http://www.youtube.com/watch?v=nSByug87_gY

minions in the media provide all the wrong answers to the deepest questions that are universally felt in the human psyche and that God wants to use to draw people to himself. We must realize that when we turn on the television, we are choosing to expose our minds to enemy propaganda. If we do not consciously recognize this influence and strongly counter it with exposure to God's Word, we can expect nothing except deception. Instead of living our lives enmeshed in the Media Matrix, we must learn to live by faith in the reality presented in the Bible.[19]

19 See Habakkuk, Hosea, or a host of other books for a much more accurate picture of what is happening to our society than that provided by television talking heads.

**Chapter 14**

# The Satanic Underground: "Aliens," Possession, Oppression, Influence, Ritual Abuse, and the Gateways that Lead There

"When you come into the land which the Lord your God is giving you, you shall not learn to follow the abominations of those nations. There shall not be found among you *anyone* who makes his son or his daughter pass through the fire, *or one* who practices witchcraft, *or* a soothsayer, or one who interprets omens, or a sorcerer, or one who conjures spells, or a medium, or a spiritist, or one who calls up the dead. For all who do these things *are* an abomination to the Lord, and because of these abominations the Lord your God drives them out from before you. You shall be blameless before the Lord your God. For these nations which you will dispossess listened to soothsayers and diviners; but as for you, the Lord your God has not appointed such for you."

—Deuteronomy 18:9-14[1]

The spiritual world, as the physical world, operates under a set of "natural laws" that God has put in place. Just as we are restricted to the limitations of gravity, the laws of thermodynamics, etc, forces in the spiritual realm also must operate under the restrictions of certain laws. Satan and his spiritual minions cannot overpower human free will and bend humanity to their aims in whatever way they desire. Satan's demonic and angelic forces[2] need gateways, they need access, and they need permission. As

1 My point with this quotation is not to associate America with Israel, but to point out that America is involved in the very same practices today that God declared to be an abomination thousands of years ago.

2 It is my tentative opinion that there is some difference between the "fallen" rebellious angels and demons but these apparent differences could be the result of different manifestations of the same entities. There certainly seems to be a difference in power among these entities in Biblical accounts such as Matthew 17:21.

with all of Satan's agenda, this permission and these gateways are sought and obtained by deception.

The Holy Spirit of God indwells a Christian's heart, the center of his or her spiritual being. Satan's evil spirits oppress and possess a person's arms, legs, and the top of their head.[3] The Holy Spirit promises death to the carnal man and brings eternal life in Christ; the evil spirits promise life to the carnal man and bring eternal death and damnation. The Holy Spirit brings humility and obedience to God; the evil spirits appeal to pride and promise power to defy or disregard God's law. The Holy Spirit asks us to become slaves to the will of Christ and thus sets us free from the power of sin; the evil spirits promise freedom and self-determination and thus enslave people to the bondage of addiction and sin. The fruit of the Holy Spirit is "love, joy, peace, longsuffering, kindness, goodness, faithfulness, gentleness, [and] self control;" the fruit of evil spirits and life in the flesh are "adultery, fornication, uncleanness, lewdness, idolatry, sorcery, hatred, contentions, jealousies, outbursts of wrath, selfish ambitions, dissensions, heresies, envy, murders, drunkenness, revelries, and the like."[4] The Holy Spirit will always lead us to read, study, and understand God's Word; evil spirits seek to block people from reading the Bible, to deny its authority and accuracy, to misinterpret, twist, take out of context, and even to ridicule God's Holy Scriptures. The Holy Spirit will always magnify Jesus Christ and cause us to grow more and more focused on Him; evil spirits will always seek to distract from, distort, minimize, dismiss, and blaspheme Jesus Christ.

Because of the clear differences between the work of the Holy Spirit and the work of fallen and demonic spirits, it may seem that satanic influence would be easy to identify, repudiate, and avoid. However, the problem is that Satan and his spiritual minions hide the gateways they seek to enter through as entertainment, enlightenment, and extraterrestrials.

Leonard Ravenhill often said, "Entertainment is the devil's substitute for joy."[5] Entertainment is also one of the devil's main

3 This statement is based on the accounts of many people who have been freed from the power and influence of these spirits and feel them leaving from these areas. Please listen to Bill Mcleod's excellent sermon "The Occult" which is available at www.sermonindex.net.

4 See Galatians 5:19-26

5 See www.ravenhill.org or www.sermonindex.net.

means of deceptively influencing and drawing the minds of men, women, and especially children into the demonic and occultic realm. Children's literature is rife with references to witchcraft, spells, and magic. For example, a search for "witchcraft" in the teen books section of Amazon turns up nearly 1,800 results.[6] A search for "Wicca" in the children's book section returns 282 results. This includes titles such as "My First Little Workbook of Wicca," "Circle of Three," and hundreds of others.[7] When the satanic elite get behind a product the way they got behind the Harry Potter phenomenon, one can be sure that there is more of a motive than just book sales.[8] The portrayal of witchcraft and sorcery as cute, funny, and harmless encourages children to dive further and further into the occult.

Comic books are another medium where occult and magical themes are pushed. Alan Moore, the creator of the heralded graphic novel titled *Watchmen*, is a "practicing magician [and] worships a Roman snake-deity named Glycon."[9] Grant Morrison is another writer of comics and another practicing magician. In a lecture given to fans he enthusiastically (and drunkenly) extols the efficacy of magic and talks about how his use of sigils has led to what he draws actually manifesting itself in reality.[10]

Nearly all entertainment produced today is at its core advertising for the satanic world system. So, it is unsurprising to find that the use of magic extends to advertising itself in the form of corporate logos. Frank Lorde writes, "The occult world is very clear about how they view the use of magic in everyday life. Call it psychology, programming, or manipulation, but do not forget to identify it as sorcery."[11] Many corporate logos function as magic

---

6 Not all of these books are supportive of witchcraft, but many are. www.amazon.com

7 Amazon.com: Children's Books -Wicca

8 Another more recent example would be the ridiculously unjustified hype and promotion of Dan Brown's inaccurate and mediocre novels.

9 Alan Moore page on Wikipedia, http://en.wikipedia.org/wiki/Alan_Moore#Personal_life

10 See "Final Crisis: The Gaia Sophia Mysteries Part II" by Frank Lorde for Grant Morrison's lecture as well as Lorde's analysis. http://wiseasserpents.com/final-crisis-the-gaia-sophia-mysteries-part-ii/

11 See "A Kind of Magic" at http://wiseasserpents.com/wise-as-serpents-a-kind-of-magic/

sigils to accomplish the purpose of tying positive associations (created through advertising) in the consumer's mind to the corporate logo and thereby the product.[12] The reason you reach for the "Tide" detergent instead of the cheaper generic (or better yet, old fashioned soap), is because of the unconscious associations that have been formed through corporate propagated sorcery. Dozens of corporate logos contain occult imagery such as pyramids, all-seeing eyes, and pentagrams which are created by the same method that magicians create sigils.[13]

Music is another key avenue by which spiritual entities seek access to young minds. Much attention has been paid to pop music's promotion of materialism and sexual immorality. However, less criticism has been leveled at the occult symbolism and ritual that is quite often present in the visual presentation and lyrical content of artists such as Madonna and Jay-Z. Madonna openly admits to practicing Kabbalah, the occult ritual system that is the root of Freemasonry rituals and symbolism.[14] In her infamous performance on MTV, Madonna didn't just promote lesbian sensuality by kissing Britney Spears and Christina Aguilera; she performed an occult Kabbalah ritual.[15] Jay-Z is a third degree Freemason who incorporated Masonic (Kabbalah) rituals and symbolism into his music video for "Run This Town" on the "Blueprint 3" album.[16] Appropriately, when Jay-Z was interviewed about the album, he wore a sweatshirt that read "Do

---

12 Ibid

13 See "Open Your Mind-Illuminati Symbolism" from Nufffrespect for visual examples of this http://www.youtube.com/watch?v=9LEljS3ib84&feature=channel_page

14 While by no means a consistently reliable source of information and analysis, Freeman's analysis of this phenomenon is quite interesting. See "Anna Nicole, Britney, and Mind Control" on Google video. http://video.google.com.au/videoplay?docid=-891321698051955222&q=mind+control+duration%3Along&pr=goog-sl#

15 "The Arrivals Part 13" http://www.youtube.com/watch?v=-VVxaxJQWD4&feature=PlayList&p=C23254B66DEDE39E&index=14 The video series as a whole is certainly not accurate (it is Muslim propaganda), but this section is interesting.

16 See "The Jay-Z Deception" on YouTube from Forerunner 777 for a complete breakdown and analysis of Jay-Z's connections to Freemasonry and symbolism incorporated in his music video. http://www.youtube.com/watch?v=PDgUTQYEIas&feature=related

What Thou Wilt." That, of course, is the infamous and blasphemous quote from avowed Satanist Aleister Crowley.[17] Whether it is called Wicca, Freemasonry, Kabbalah, Luciferianism, Satanism, or a variety of other terms; it is all sorcery; it is all the worship of false gods; and it is all abhorred by God.

Pop artists such as Britney Spears are often the products of trauma based mind control and conditioning.[18] Trauma based mind control is closely connected with Satanic Ritual Abuse (SRA). SRA involves the process of inflicting so much pain on a child that the child must either disassociate or die. The disassociation creates split, or multiple, personalities. These personalities can then be programmed to be anything from sex slaves to assassins to pop music stars.[19] The programming starts to break down around the age of 30. So, it is no surprise to see women like Britney Spears or Anna Nicole Smith "go crazy" in what is really an attempt to break out of their conditioning. There is a lot of emphasis placed on blond hair and blue eyes among the corrupt elites who are in control of these projects. What appears to be just celebrity eccentricity, such as Britney Spears dying her hair brown or shaving her head, is evidence that she is trying to escape her handlers. If, as certainly appears to be the case, Britney Spears is mind-controlled and her programming is beginning to break down, it is unlikely that her handlers will let her live for very much longer.[20]

While some sympathy can be felt for exploited and controlled girls such as Britney Spears, it certainly appears that some artists, such as Madonna and Jay-Z, carry out their occult agenda quite willingly and enthusiastically. Regardless of the level of

---

17 This clip can be seen in "The Jay-Z Deception" part 5. http://www.youtube.com/watch?v=H6gxinWFylY&feature=channel

18 See "Anna Nicole, Britney, and Mind Control" on Google video. http://video.google.com.au/videoplay?docid=-8913216980519552228&q=mind+control+duration%3Along&pr=goog-sl#

19 For further reading on this subject, read *The Illuminati Formula to Create an Undetectable Total Mind Controlled Slave* by Fritz Springmeier and Cisco Wheeler, available at http://www.theforbiddenknowledge.com/hardtruth/illuminati_formula_mind_control.htm . Also see survivor accounts from Cathy O'Brien and Brice Taylor in *Trance Formation of America* and *Thanks for the Memories...The Truth Has Set Me Free*, respectively.

20 Russ Dizdar has worked with victims of Satanic Ritual Abuse for many years as part of his evangelistic and deliverance ministry. Check out his work at www.shatterthedarkness.net.

manipulation by human handlers and programmers, however, most of the music industry is manipulated on the spiritual level in demonic attempts to open gateways into young minds through messages ("Do What Thou Wilt") and symbolism.

The harmful messages of movies are legion and to some degree have been well analyzed and critiqued by the Christian community. All of the "gateway" occult messages that are found in books and music are found to an even greater degree in movies. However, one message that is beginning to be put forward in more and more films that has not often been critiqued is variations on the theory of Panspermia; the idea that life on Earth has its origins in outer space. Evolution is still ostensibly the consensus view among scientists. However, its days are numbered as the intricacies of DNA are revealed and Darwinistic evolution continues to accumulate theoretical holes faster than its supporters can come up with pseudo-evidence.[21]

Panspermia, then, is the next big thing. It is not particularly convincing as a scientific theory and totally bankrupt as far as settling the issue of whether there is a Creator of the universe. Panspermia would simply move the creation of life back a step. However, this relatively new theory is being marketed by Hollywood as the new and trendy way to deny God His rightful recognition as Creator. Films that posit an alien or extraterrestrial source of life, or "ancient astronauts" manipulating life, include *Mission to Mars* (aimed at kids with a G rating), *In Search of Ancient Astronauts, Battlestar Galactica, Stargate, The Fourth Kind,* and *A Genesis Found*. Through these films as well as other sources in ufology (i.e. Erich von Daniken and Zecharia Sitchin) and conspiracy circles, people are quickly "discovering" and repeating the idea that we are an alien genetic-alteration project or some version of that idea. The idea that aliens may be responsible for the origin of mankind is becoming more popular in underground circles. Concurrently, the idea that aliens are currently interacting with certain enlightened members of humanity and may become even more involved in the near future is also deceiving more and more people.

The New Age Movement and ufology enthusiasts share many beliefs and the membership of these groups has a lot of overlap.

21 See the excellent breakdown of Panspermia at http://www.alienresistance.org/panspermia.htm

Those that have had contact with what they believe to be aliens, without fail, report that the aliens are teaching them a belief system quite similar to the New Age Movement. This belief system is consistently anti-Christian. The emphasis is always on man reaching a higher plane, or a higher level of consciousness, and on those wonderful aliens, or ascended masters, who just want to help mankind. The emphasis of this help is to point out that there is no sin and no need for Jesus Christ to be our Lord and Savior. Pastor and ufology researcher Guy Malone puts it this way:

> According to all modern accounts, the so-called "aliens" being reported today teach doctrines that are in 180 degree opposition to the Bible - just as false gods and fallen angels always have. Would intelligent beings travel the cosmos solely to discredit one religion? The angelic understanding of Genesis 6 (and texts from almost all ancient cultures), combined with the fact that abductions are stopped in Jesus' name places a new burden on the ufologist to PROVE that these are authentic beings from other worlds, rather than fallen angels.[22]

The alien abduction phenomenon must be understood in its spiritual context. The extraterrestrial explanations of aliens (beings from other planets with advanced technology) fall apart with a proper understanding of physics as well as the unlikely anti-Jesus Christ agenda. Even more unreasonable, however, is to develop the skeptic/materialist standpoint that all of the thousands or even millions of people are making up stories independently that just happen to mirror each other. What, exactly, would their motivation be? To have everyone think they are crazy? One explanation takes all of the data and puts it in a coherent framework: that this is one more battlefield of the spiritual war that the Bible says is going on all around us and has been for thousands of years.

Satan always counterfeits the works of Jesus Christ and twists and distorts the truth of God's Word. His "alien" minions and New Age gurus tell people that they each are special and have a special calling in life. This specialness and calling, however, are based not on the price paid by Jesus Christ, but by some inherent

22 This Guy Malone quote is from the excellent website www.alienresistance.org in the "Every Knee Shall Bow" section. http://www.alienresistance.org/alienufoflyer.htm

individual merit or special talent. The evil and deceptive spirits promise that enlightenment or even godhood awaits the individual who will listen to them and follow their teachings. There is a spiritual vacuum created by decades of materialistic worldview in western societies. Because of this, many people are susceptible to buying into any spiritual experience that they encounter— without analyzing where it comes from, or considering the possibility that not all spiritual experience is a good thing. The New Age teaching about the "Christ Consciousness" and all the rest of the "new" teachings about Jesus Christ fail the test given to us in Scripture.

> Beloved, do not believe every spirit, but test the spirits, whether they are of God; because many false prophets have gone out into the world. By this you know the Spirit of God: Every spirit that confesses that Jesus Christ has come in the flesh is of God, and every spirit that does not confess that Jesus Christ has come in the flesh is not of God. And this is the *spirit* of Antichrist, which you have heard was coming, and is now already in the world.[23]

Satan craves control over the hearts and minds of men. His ultimate goal is usurpation of Jesus Christ's rightful position as king over all the earth. The Kingdom of God is built through humility, love, and freedom from the power of sin through Jesus Christ. Satan builds his kingdom through deception, manipulation, and enslaving people to sin. Satan's ultimate goal is not just that people will turn away from God or deny God in the first place; it is that people will worship him as god. All of the entertainment programming described above is ultimately designed to get people started down a path that ends in worshipping Satan.

Satanic Ritual Abuse (SRA) is what the cultists, druids, secret society members, certain sections of the military, Gaia worshippers, etc, ultimately end up participating in if they travel far enough down their respective paths.[24] Satanism consists of a

23 I John 4:1-3

24 The path to Satanism is much more direct in some of these groups than others. Most Satanic Ritual Abuse is passed down and carried on generationally. Kay Griggs, wife of Colonel George Griggs, gives an extended and in-depth interview about the revelations of this environment in the higher levels of the military. http://video.google.com/videoplay?docid=-341031042963487862#

blasphemous and wicked counterfeiting of Christianity through perverting and inverting God's sacrifice of His only Son, Jesus Christ. The same satanic rituals performed in ancient Egypt are still practiced today.[25]

The thousands of children who have testified to being victims of SRA recount similar accounts of rituals from all over America and other countries including Canada, England, France, and Italy.[26] The books and articles cited in this section contain children's accounts (and pictures) of these rituals, but the rituals' explicit, nauseating, and gory details will not be discussed here.[27] SRA always involves blood sacrifice. Famous Satanist Aleister Crowley explained the reason for this in his book *Magick*.

> The blood is the life. This simple statement is explained by the Hindus by saying that the blood is the principle vehicle of vital Prana.... It was the theory of the ancient Magicians, that any living being is a storehouse of energy varying in quantity according to the size and health of the animal, and in quality according to its mental and moral character. At the death of the animal this energy is liberated suddenly. [For Magical purposes] The animal should therefore be killed within the Circle, or the Triangle, as the case may be, so that its energy cannot escape. An animal should be selected whose nature accords with that of the ceremony...For the highest spiritual working one must accordingly choose that victim which contains the greatest and purest force. A male child of perfect innocence and high intelligence is the most satisfactory and suitable victim... Those magicians who object to the use of blood have endeavoured [sic] to replace it with incense... But the bloody sacrifice, though more dangerous is more efficacious; and for nearly all purposes human sacrifice is the best.[28]

---

25 *The Egyptian Masonic-Satanic-Connection* by David L. Carrico and Donna M. Carrico covers this in chapter 6, "Egyptian Satanism." http://ritualabuse.us/ritualabuse/books/chapters-from-the-egyptian-masonic-satanic-connection/

26 "Satanic Ritual Abuse" http://www.the7thfire.com/new_world_order/Freemasonry/satanic_ritual_abuse.htm

27 There has been a concerted effort to refute and explain away the thousands of reports of SRA. However, the propagation of "false memory syndrome" as an explanation requires far more credulity than to believe that these reports are based on real events.

28 http://ritualabuse.us/ritualabuse/books/chapters-from-the-egyptian-masonic-satanic-connection/

SRA victims are required to drink blood and to participate in spilling the blood of others.[29] SRA victims also recount being required to participate in bathing in blood as well as cannibalizing the intestines and the heart.[30] It is clear that these rituals are both counterfeiting the cleansing blood of Jesus Christ and deliberately defying as many of God's prohibitions as possible.

Satanic rituals also involve perverse and violent sexual activities directed mainly at children.[31] Other rituals include covering children in urine and feces, dismemberment, upside-down crucifixions, and peeling the skin off of babies.[32] The horrors of all this are difficult to comprehend or imagine, but they reveal Satan's true agenda and the ultimate in rebellion against God. Alex Jones has commented many times to the effect that the elite believe they are going beyond good and evil and that their destruction of innocent life is in their eyes a necessary step towards ultimate control and their New World Order.[33]

Russ Dizdar is an expert in the occult, New Age, and satanic subculture in the United States. He cites the number of 4.5 million cases of SRA and has dealt with many victims personally through his ministry and his work with a police department on a taskforce dealing with occult crime.[34] He experienced the New Age and occult lifestyle for himself before he was saved by Jesus Christ. He emphasizes the power of Jesus Christ to overcome all of the finite spiritual powers of darkness. Dizdar believes that the New Agers pursuit of "spiritual places" all around the world (i.e. Mayan pyramids, ziggurats, Egyptian pyramids, Bohemian Grove, etc.), is a result of the drawing of evil spirits in preparation for greater and greater manifestations of spiritual power.[35] The "satanic chosen ones" have gone through hundreds of rituals

29 *The Egyptian Masonic-Satanic-Connection* by David L. Carrico and Donna M. Carrico covers this in chapter 7, "Satanic Ritual Abuse," which was contributed by Rick Doniger.

30 Ibid

31 Ibid

32 Ibid

33 *The Alex Jones Show* is available at www.infowars.com

34 "Satanic Rituals in the USA" by Russ Dizdar is available at http://www.shatterthedarkness.net/ Pastor Dizdar is also the author of *The Black Awakening*.

35 Ibid

each and they are now "sleepers" who are ready to activate and do the will of Satan. They are designed to attack pastors and other Christians who they view as a threat at a spiritual level. They use the carrots of power and money to get government leaders to participate in rituals that place oppressive and manipulative spiritual forces on them.[36]

One of the satanic rituals Dizdar exposes is the "marriage to the beast" ritual that takes place on September 7th. This involves the laying of a young girl on a table with men in black robes who sexually abuse the girl in order to complete the ritual. The programming of the girl who Russ Dizdar worked with was to pour gasoline on herself and set herself on fire in service to her mother, a satanic priestess, on her 15th birthday. In the aftermath of another ritual, Dizdar, while working with a police department, saw a head on a table in which the girl's face and scalp had been peeled off so that all that was left was a pink head.[37]

It may seem unbelievable that these horrors are taking place in America. However, when we take a historical and Biblical view it is clear that this ultimate expression of wickedness and rebellion against God is found concurrently with the worship of false gods, sexual immorality, and sorcery. Our society seems less wicked to us than many of the societies described in the Bible. Not because it is less wicked, but because we view our society through our own eyes, while in the Bible we read how God views wickedness. The path of unabated hedonism and greed, along with the worship of false gods, leads to a Sodom and Gomorrah-like culture. A similar fate to that of those infamous cities awaits America if the Holy Spirit does not bring repentance and spiritual revival.

36 Ibid
37 Ibid

# Chapter 15

# Reality.

"Jesus said to him, 'I am the way, the truth, and the life. No one comes to the Father except through Me.'"

—John 14:6

In this chapter, I will discuss why I wrote this book and the extent to which I believe knowing about these issues is important. My goal is not to inspire new conspiracy theorists. My intention is to expose how corrupt, bankrupt, and insidious the kingdoms of men are in this world. Hopefully, this knowledge will inspire you to seek the Kingdom of God. In my own journey into this information I have found that no matter what road I go down, I find over and over again that truth is found in God's Word and in Jesus Christ alone. There is no theology, conspiracy theory, or understanding of the world that Satan and our flesh can't twist into something harmful. This can only be avoided if we focus our eyes and hearts on Jesus Christ and prayerfully allow our interpretation to be filtered through the discernment made available by the Holy Spirit. My hope and prayer is that this book gives you a different lens through which to view the world and that this new lens spurs you to rely wholly on Jesus Christ.

If we look at the history of the early church we see that they were persecuted, mocked, rejected, and sometimes ultimately killed for their Christian faith. Despite these adverse circumstances, they were not confused by the world in which they lived. They viewed their lives in the context of a spiritual war. There was no cause greater than the building of the Kingdom of God.

Christians of the early church expected to be hated and persecuted because of their love for Jesus Christ.

We must realize that nothing has changed. We do not live in a Christian nation. Political power is by definition diametrically opposed to the Kingdom of God. Political power is far more harmful to Christianity when it is wielded by the supposed church than in cases of open persecution of Christians by the state. The power of the state has normally increased concurrently with the misery of the people contained within. Until Christ comes and claims His right to rule; we must peacefully but unwaveringly resist the tyranny that Satan intends to inflict on this world. Resistance to satanic tyranny can be expressed in obedience to God through prayer, worship, and love.

> Put on the whole armor of God, that you may be able to stand against the wiles of the devil. For we do not wrestle against flesh and blood, but against principalities, against powers, against the rulers of the darkness of this age, against spiritual *hosts* of wickedness in the heavenly *places*. Therefore take up the whole armor of God, that you may be able to withstand in the evil day, and having done all, to stand.[1]

In the spiritual war that we are all in, prayer is both a defensive and offensive weapon. One of Satan's biggest lies to Christians is that prayer does not matter. This lie is often ensconced in poorly taught theology about God's omnipotence. The Bible, the biographies of Christians, and our own experience make it clear that for reasons beyond our understanding, God has ordered the universe in such a way that through our prayers God's will is manifested in miraculous ways all around us.

Evidence for prayer's efficacy includes the reaction of our spiritual enemies when we decide to pray. When I attempt the spend time in prayer, there are immediate and ongoing temptations and distractions that race through my brain.[2] Satan and his spiritual minions want us to think about things we have to do, think about that person we like or dislike, think about how tired we are, to think about anything else except our Lord and Savior Jesus Christ.

---

1 Ephesians 6:11-13

2 Paul Washer's advice to pray until you can pray and then pray until you're done praying is certainly relevant in this situation.

Prayer changes our hearts as well as being used by God to influence the world around us. It is impossible to pray and harbor hate and unforgiveness in our hearts towards those around us. It is impossible to commune with God Almighty and maintain a prideful spirit and attitude. Through time spent with Jesus Christ, He teaches us to view the world, other people, ourselves, sin, etc, as He sees them—not as the world sees. This Kingdom of God mindset is one of the many benefits of a prayerful walk with God.

> I *am* the Lord your God, who brought you out of the land of Egypt, out of the house of bondage. You shall have no other gods before me. You shall not make for yourself a carved image—any likeness *of anything* that *is* in heaven above, or that *is* in the earth beneath, or that *is* in the water under the earth; you shall not bow down to them nor serve them. For I, the Lord your God, *am* a jealous God.[3]

Worship is another activity that is given preeminence by God in His Word. God has made it abundantly clear that we are to worship Him alone. Lucifer and the angels that went with him rebelled at least in part because he desired that we worship him along with God. The teaching that God and Lucifer are equals is still present in Freemasonic, Gnostic, and other Luciferian belief systems today.[4] One of Satan's biggest carrots for his minions is the opportunity to become the object of worship. In other words, they become idols. Satan is attempting to use technology and manipulation of the leaders of this world to bring the whole world into a system of absolute control. So, that he can inhabit the leader supernaturally and compel worship from all mankind. This is a counterfeit version of what Paul promises will happen when Jesus Christ is revealed in all of His glory.

> Therefore God also has highly exalted Him and given Him the name which is above every name, that at the name of Jesus every knee should bow, of those in heaven, and of those on earth, and of

3 Exodus 20:2-5a

4 These Gnostic teachings are then of course subtly propagated throughout our culture through Hollywood and the rest of the mass media. See the documentary "Hollywood's War on God" by Pastor Joe Schimmel for analysis of many examples of this. http://hollywoodswar.com/home.html

those under the earth, and *that* every tongue should confess that Jesus Christ is Lord, to the glory of God the Father.[5]

One of the perversions that took place in the Catholic Church was to elevate Mary and certain saints to a level where they are to be worshipped and prayed to by Christians. There is no Biblical support for this teaching whatsoever, of course. In fact, even the angels stridently point out that they are not to be worshipped whenever they encounter people in the Bible.[6]

As Christians, we must learn again that worship really matters. Worship is not entertainment for us on a Sunday morning. Worship is a powerful spiritual force that empowers the recipient of worship to work in the hearts of the worshippers. This is true whether we worship Yahweh or the false gods of this world. Turn on the television, go to a pop music concert, observe a political convention, attend an Earth Day celebration, and you will see people worshipping. They are just not worshipping God. We tend to follow the example of those we worship, or "idolize." Christian leaders often bemoan the "secularization" of American culture. Secularization is not the problem; idol worship is the problem. Is not the elevation of the well-being of "Mother Earth" (Gaia) above the lives of men, women, and children worship? Do not the tear-stained faces of Obama supporters on the night he won the election reveal hearts of idol worship?[7] What about adolescent girls who get to see their favorite pop star, or middle aged men who cheer for their favorite football team?

Human beings are designed to worship. If we do not direct our worship solely on God, we cannot help but worship false gods. If we recognize the reality and importance of worship, we will be much more careful about who we worship. By worshipping God, and God alone, we recognize the true order of the universe and give God access to our hearts in order to continue to draw us closer to Him.

5 Philippians 2:9-11

6 Revelation 19:10 is one of several examples of this.

7 "President-Elect Barack Obama on Election Night" http://www.youtube.com/watch?v=HfHbw3n0EIM There are also examples of people praying to Obama. See "People PRAY to Obama...Deliver us Obama!!" http://www.youtube.com/watch?v=dcKbfJJFClk

> You shall love the Lord your God with all your heart, with all your soul, and with all your mind. This is the first and greatest commandment. And the second is like it. You shall love your neighbor as yourself. On these two commandments hang all the Law and the Prophets.[8]

Love is at the heart of what our lives as Christians are to be about. We are born with an innate need to be loved. Sin is often disguised as an opportunity to receive love. As with everything he does, Satan offers a counterfeit version of God's love. Instead of humbling ourselves and begging God for a spirit of repentance, Satan wants us to seek love and affection by our own merit. Like all of Satan's deceptions, following this path of seeking love and affirmation from others by trying to impress, woo, or otherwise earn it in our own strength leaves us feeling rejected, unloved, and vulnerable to temptation. God's love is not a reward for a job well done. God's love is a gift that we are not even capable of receiving, much less earning, without His mighty work of redemption. God's love does not depend on circumstances. In fact, it is often easier to receive the love of God when we are hurting and broken. The ultimate expression of love is of course Christ's death on the cross and His endurance of the cup of God's wrath poured out upon Him in all of its terrible and holy justice.

> A new commandment I give to you, that you love one another; as I have loved you, that you also love one another. By this all will know that you are My disciples, if you have love for one another.[9]

Jesus Christ tells us that others will identify us as Christ-followers by our love for one another. How do we make love the distinctive characteristic of our lives? I believe that we must be able to receive God's love before we can truly love other people. To love others, we must learn to see them as Christ sees each one of us; as someone He loved so unconditionally and sacrificially that He took our sin upon Himself. When we view each other in this way, there is no room for judgment. The relative morality, talent, or self-efficacy of each of us to each other is irrelevant. The only thing worth considering when we look at each other

8 Matthew 22:37-40
9 John 13:34-35

is that Christ loved that person enough to suffer God's wrath in his or her place. It is only when we view people through this lens that we are capable of loving our fellow human beings. We do not love each other because of our respective lovability, but because God bestowed inestimable worth on each of His children through the life, death, and resurrection of His Son.

There is nothing real, true, or good apart from Jesus Christ and the grace of God. Without Jesus Christ renewing our hearts and minds we are doomed to lives of deception and wickedness in this world. Everything in this world is empty and temporal apart from Jesus Christ. In Jesus Christ, "we live and move and have our being."[10] Nothing else matters.

10 Acts 17:28